AMERICAN OIL CANS
Identification and Price Guide ™
Volume 1

By Tom and Susan Allen

AMERICAN OIL CANS Identification & Price Guide ™ Volume 1

First Edition, First Printing 2003

Copyright © 2003 by Tom Allen and Susan Allen

All rights reserved. No part of this work may be reproduced or used in any form or by any means - graphic, electronic, or mechanical, including photocopying or information storage and retrieval systems excepting in the case of brief passages embodied in articles and reviews and the item number and description of individual cans which collectors are encouraged to use for their private, non commercial hobby use - without written permission from the copyright holder.

Library of Congress Cataloging in Publication Data

Allen, Tom, 1963-
    American oil cans : identification & price guide / Tom Allen & Susan Allen.
        v. : col. ill. ; 22 x 29 cm.
        includes bibliographical references.
        ISBN 0-9728607-0-3   Library of Congress Control Number: 2003090747
        i. Allen, Susan. 1. Oilcans-United States-Caltalogs. 2. Oilcans-Collectors and collecting-Catalogs.
        NK8459.054
        629.255

Written by Tom Allen and Susan Allen
Edited by Tom Allen and Susan Allen

Published by   Dean's Books, Inc.
                   1426 S. Kansas Ave.
                   Topeka, KS 66612
                   Phone: 785-357-4708

Email: contact@oilcanbook.com
Website: www.oilcanbook.com

Printed and bound in the United States of America.

Contents

Acknowledgments and Disclaimer 4

How to use this book 5

Grading cans 6

Pricing cans 6-7

A very short history of sealed cans 7

Dating cans 8-9

Examples of lids and seams 10-13

Before and After photos 14

Key 15

Can Identification Text and Photos 16-99

Pennsylvania Grade Crude Oil Association membership list 100-126

Bibliography 127

Notes 128

Acknowledgments

The authors would like to thank the following people who provided cans and/or information included in this volume. Without their help, the book you see before you could not have been produced.

Michael Allen
Robert Bailey
Jerry Chapman
Tim Dye
Bob Ehinger
Randy Heldenbrand
Wayne Henderson
Mike Jones
Ed Love
Jim Masson
Kent McCullough
Sam McIntyre
W. Clark Miller
Mike Odell
John Pearson
Norm Pennie
Don Raleigh
Craig Stater
Fred Stoke

Disclaimer

The text and products pictured in this book are from the collection of the authors, or from the collections of those listed above. The information contained within is not sponsored, endorsed, or otherwise affiliated with any of the companies whose products are presented herein. The information provided in this book was derived from the independent research of the authors.

How to use this book

All cans are indexed by the brand name. However, the index is not exactly alphabetical. Certain liberties were taken to keep some related cans together. Primarily though, the first thing you read on a can is what it is listed under. Every can is cross referenced with all other cans produced by the same company. On the bottom of each page of text is a cross reference listing all other cans associated with any particular can. As an example, #300 Falcon, made by Oscar Bryant, is cross referenced with #980 Swift which is also a brand of Oscar Bryant.

For collectors of 1 quart cans, a small box below each photo has been provided to be used as a check off to indicate cans already in your collection. If condition is important, you may wish to place a number inside the box to indicate the condition of the can in your collection. Should you choose to do this, I suggest using a pencil so you can easily change the number as the can is upgraded. For more information on grading, see the section on how to grade oil cans.

For collectors of 4 and 5 quart cans, small 4's and 5's have been placed to the right of each check off box indicating that the above can is known in a 4 and/or 5 quart size. This eliminates needless duplication (since almost all 4 and 5 quarts are exact copies of 1 quarts except for their size) and allows more cans to be shown in each volume. Should a previously unknown 4 or 5 quart example be discovered, simply update the book by adding the appropriate number to the right of the check off box. The check off box can be used for 4 and 5 quarts the same way as described above for 1 quarts.

For help in identifying some Pennsylvania grade oil cans, a listing of identified membership numbers for oil companies belonging to the Pennsylvania Grade Crude Oil Association is provided on pages 100-126. Some cans and also a number of signs only mention a brand name of oil and not any mention of what company produced it or where it is located. If the company was a member of the P.G.C.O.A. and the advertisement was for a Pennsylvania grade of oil, the P.G.C.O.A. logo and membership number would be shown as well. Using the P.G.C.O.A. membership list can help identify signs and cans which have no manufacturer indicated. As additional member companies are discovered, their membership numbers will be included in future volumes.

Grading cans

Grading of oil cans, as with most collectibles, is subjective at best. I'll give some basic thoughts about grading. If a scale of 1 to 10 is used, with 10 being the best, most collectors will look for cans in at least a grade of 7 condition. Lesser condition cans are usually passed over unless they are extremely rare or are priced considerably cheaper. Even then, lesser condition cans are looked at as "fillers" until a more displayable example is acquired. It should be noted that cans in grade 10 are few and far between. Due to cans being packaged 24 to a case, the normal wear a can acquires from rubbing against other cans in a case almost always lowers a can to a grade 9. This grade is typically the grade most collectors aim for.

Some collectors have asked what effect emptying a can has on it's grade. Most collectors feel draining a can by poking two small holes in the bottom should not affect it's grade. Some collectors even prefer this because for several reasons. If a full can is left sitting long enough, it may begin to leak which leads to an oily mess all over the shelf and anything on lower shelves. The oil may also damage the paint on the can. Also, an empty can is much cheaper to ship. Another reason is that if you accidentally drop a full can, it will dent. If you drop an empty can, it is more likely to bounce causing less damage to the can.

Recently, with the discovery of canning machines and leftover old stock lids, the ability to re-lid cans has become available. A can that has been re-lidded with the exact same style of lid (including some form of SAE designation) should be graded only slightly lower and in most collectors opinion should be considered practically equal to a can with it's original lid provided no additional damage to the can has occurred from the re-lidding. It is these authors' opinions that poorly re-lidded cans should be graded significantly lower. Improper lids would include lids that don't match the style of the bottom lid, or a lid that doesn't match the era of the can such as a 1970's style lid attached to a 1930's style can. A more common mistake is to use a lid with no SAE number for the top of a can. Practically all 1950's and older oil cans had some type of embossed weight designation in the lid. This same criteria can be applied to replaced bottom lids on cans with exception to the SAE designation since the bottoms were always unmarked. It should be noted that ATF and antifreeze cans almost always had plain lids and bottoms.

Pricing cans

The price of a can is effected the most by two factors. Those being supply and demand. Beyond this, there are several other factors that affect a can's value.

1.) Graphics. Often called "picture cans", cans with detailed graphics on them typically bring a higher price. Most of the highest priced cans fall into the category of picture cans. Although many corporate logos such as Mobil's pegasus, can be considered a graphic, it's cans with a true picture on them such as the Sooner Queen can pictured on page 81 that have the highest value. This isn't to say an attractive logo cannot command a high price. An example of this are the Frontier cans shown on page 41. The Frontier oil company's logo of a cowboy on a bucking horse is quite popular with collectors. This increased demand because of their popular logo combined with their relative scarcity increases their value. Just having a colorful graphic or logo doesn't guarantee a higher value. The best example of this are two cans from the Oscar Bryant Oil company in Hollis, Oklahoma. Their two brands, Falcon and Swift, both of which are pictured in this volume are colorful cans, but are so common they have a very low value compared to what you would expect from looking at them.

2.) 4 and 5 quart sizes. 5 quart cans usually bring slightly higher prices than quarts and 4 quart cans usually sell for the same or less than quart cans. These two sizes of cans were designed to contain a full oil change in one can. The 5 quart size was produced until the late 1950's when the majority of cars began needing 4 quarts for a full change. 5 quarts are more popular since, in the time frame they were produced, many more brands of oil were being made. By the 1950's, when the 4 quart size became popular, only the large oil companies remained and their can designs had become less graphic than their designs of the 1930's and 40's.

3.) Regional factor: Unlike today, during the 1930's up through the 1950's, there were a large number of small oil companies that marketed in limited areas. Cans from these small companies often command a higher price in the areas where they were sold and were best remembered. There are exceptions to this as well. One of the best known being a brand of oil called Oilzum marketed by the White and Bagley company primarily in the northeastern U.S. These cans feature the head of a race car driver with his racing goggles pulled up over his hat. These attractive cans are sought after by collectors all over the U.S.

4.) Rarity: Obviously the more rare a can is, the better the chance of it's value increasing. Here I want to cover a few factors that make a can more rare and thus generally higher in value. The type of oil will affect a can's value. I'm not referring to different weights of oil but rather what type of transportation it's used in. Cans which indicate that they are for use specifically in airplanes, boats or motorcycles are generally more difficult to find due to the relatively small number of these cans that were produced compared to cans made for cars and trucks. It should be noted that it must be indicated on the face of the can that it is for a motorcycle, airplane or boat for this to be true. If the can's usage is identified on the lid only and the face of the can is the same as a regular can then there is no appreciable difference in value. Round sealed quart cans used for boats are especially difficult to find. Most oil packaged for boats was sold in cans with resealable screw caps. These were what most boat owners would buy since a boat would usually require less than a full quart and with a resealable can, the remainder could be kept without fear of the oil becoming contaminated or spilling. The round sealed style of outboard quart can was almost exclusively used by boat dealers or repair shops. Very few of this style of can survived.

5.) Discount Gas Station Brands: Cans from small discount brands are typically some of the most difficult to obtain. Discount marketers such as Site and Spur had small marketing territories and relatively few stations compared to national brands like Mobil and Texaco which had large numbers of stations and were also commonly sold at auto parts stores and department stores as well. The typical customer who bought his gas from a discount station would buy a quart if he was low, fill his car, then dump the can in the trash at the station. Very rarely were full quart cans of oil bought from discount stations and brought home to set in the garage for some lucky collector to find. Most oil bought at discount chains to be taken home was purchased in 2 gallon containers.

A very short history of sealed quart cans

Factory sealed quart oil cans came about largely because of three problems. Prior to sealed quart cans, most oil was sold out of bulk oil drums or in cans with screw on lids. Both of these methods of distribution had their problems. Unscrupulous gas station operators would charge you for the best quality oil but instead substitute a cheaper oil. Also common was to short change the customer by not giving them a full quart. Contamination was also a problem with bulk oil. A factory sealed can guaranteed that the consumer received a full quart of oil, that the oil was the same quality as what was identified on the outside of the can, and that the oil was not contaminated.

Sealed quart cans made from various materials were used from the mid 1930's up until the mid 1980's when the plastic bottle that is still used today came into widespread use.

Dating sealed 1, 4, and 5 quart cans

Very few cans are dated, therefore, identifying when a can was marketed is generally a rough guess at best. Three factors in identifying a can's age are the type of material from which it is made, what type of seam is used, and what style of lid it has. The very earliest factory sealed quart cans were canned in fruit tins such as peach cans. This lasted for a very short period of time. Sometime around 1932, the design we think of as a sealed quart can became the standard and by 1934, basically all sealed quarts were using this style can.

Most of the cans listed in this book are dated by using some of the tips below and on the following pages, as well as the lid and seam designs on the following pages, to ROUGHLY date them by decade. This works for one, four, and five quart cans.

A can that is listed as 1940's could have been used in the late 1930's or perhaps the early 1950's as well. The majority of the time, the can was considered to be used in the 1940's When a can has a single date listed, the date indicates either the date the can was first introduced or an actual date that appears on the can.

Dating cans by material

The first sealed quarts were produced in steel and remained that way until the WWII era. During WWII, most marketers substituted sealed glass jars for steel cans as steel had become needed for the war effort. Some oil companies chose to experiment at this time with the first composite cans. Unlike the composites of the 60's, 70's and 80's, these cans were narrower and taller than steel cans measuring 3 5/8 inches in diameter by 7 5/8 inches tall and had cardboard lids and bottoms. After the war, steel cans returned to the prominence they held before the war. Steel continued to be used almost exclusively throughout the 1940's and 50's. Steel was used as late as the early 1980's by some marketers. Aviation oil for jet airplanes is still packaged in round steel one quart cans. During the 1950's, the thickness of the steel used in cans was reduced and ribbed sides were added to help keep cans resistant to crushing. This was an important point for oil companies since the more resistant a can was to crushing, the higher the cases could be stacked which reduced the amount of warehouse floor space needed.

Beginning in the late 1950's, aluminum began being used as a cost saving measure by some marketers. Shipping being a substantial cost for oil companies, a savings of just a few cents on the shipping costs for a case of oil, multiplied by the thousands of cases shipped would add up to considerable savings. Aluminum cans were not very popular with bulk oil dealers because the thin aluminum cans crushed easily when stacked too high so more floor space was required than with steel cans.

In 1962, a new style of composite oil can was introduced. Unlike the WWII version, this style of composite can used steel lids and bottoms. This new style of composite can, being cheaper to produce, quickly became popular with many oil marketers and steadily took over the sealed quart can market replacing steel and aluminum cans. Composite cans remained the can of choice until the introduction of the plastic bottle in the 1980's.

Plastic sealed quarts were used by a small number of oil companies primarily during the late 1960's and early 1970's on an experimental basis. The cans were made from a single piece of plastic capped by a steel lid. The only marketer to use them extensively was Gulf.

Dating specific brands of cans

Amoco:
> Sometime around 1953, Amoco began dating their cans. The last four numbers in the code designate the month and year that design was introduced. For example, a code with the last four numbers 0872 was introduced in August, 1972

Esso:
> Prior to 1949: Standard Oil Company of..., 1949-1959: Esso Standard Oil Co., 1960-1972: Humble Oil and Refining Co., Beginning in July 1963, Humble began using a code consisting of either the letters S, N, or H, followed by either a 1, 2, or 3 to designate the division and the brand of oil. With design changes and formula changes a suffix letter was added to the code.

Mobil:
> 1930-1955: Socony Vacuum Oil Company, 1955-1966: Socony-Mobil Oil Company, 1966-on: Mobil Oil Corporation

Sunoco:
> Beginning in 1937, all Sunoco cans are dated.

Texaco:
> Beginning in 1954, all Texaco cans are dated with the month and year (i.e.: 5-68).

Other tips for dating cans

P.G.C.O.A. logo:
> The logo of the Pennsylvania Grade Crude Oil Association was primarily included on cans made prior to WWII, but a few companies used the logo on cans up into the early 1960's.

"Refinery Sealed":
> This term, along with phrases relating to "no substitutions" and "full measure" were used in the earliest years of sealed quarts when the practice of substituting lesser quality oil and shorting the amount given to a customer were relatively common problems.

API service grades:
> The American Petroleum Institute instituted grading of motor oil in 1952 using two letter grades such as DM, DS, MM and MS.

Company logos:
> Company logos can be used to identify the era of a can. Companies often change their logos, sometimes only slightly. These changes can be used to help date a can. An excellent reference book for use in this area is "Guide to Gasoline Logos", written by Wayne Henderson and Scott Benjamin. This is an invaluable tool for any can collector to own.

Postal Zones:
> Postal zones were established in 1943 to help in mail delivery in the largest US cities. One or two digit numbers were added after the city in an address, such as 123 Main St., Philadelphia 5 PA. These were used until the advent of the 5 digit zip code in 1963.

Zip Codes:
> 5 digit zip codes were first introduced in 1963.

Bar Codes and Uniform Product Codes (UPC)
> Bar Codes and UPC's were first used in 1973 to facilitate computer checkout in retail businesses.

Examples of lids and seams for use in dating quart oil cans

1930's
Fig. 1   This style of lid with three fat rings is used on the earliest quarts from the mid 1930's.
Fig. 2   Flat lids like this were used on brands where there was a need for more area on which to emboss writing.
Fig. 3   Another example of the flat style lid. A few very early quarts had directions embossed on the lid as to where to punch your vent hole and from where to pour.
Fig. 4   This version had two fat embossed rings with a raised center section.
Note: Some cans from the 1930's used the terms light, medium, or heavy along with, or in place of, a viscosity weight number.

1930's and 40's
Fig. 5, 6   This popular design has a single fat ring on the outside edge which gave a large area to use for embossing information. This style of lid is usually seen on cans from the late 1930's and early 1940's.
Fig. 7   Difficult to read, this lid has printed on it, "OPS RETAIL CEILING PRICE 40 CENTS PER QUART TYPE S" The OPS (office of price stabilization) controlled retail prices during World War II to help control inflation. Any can that mentions this is from the World War II era.
Fig. 8, 9   Used during the 1940's, this two ringed design was popular with many different oil companies. Figure 9 shows an uncommon style of lid with a stamped S.A.E. number. This style of lid was used extensively as a bottom without any embossing.
Fig. 10   This bottom is a common style used in the 1930's and 40's. It comes in a silver or gold color. The C in the center is the logo of the can manufacturer.

1950's and 60's
Fig. 11, 12   These totally flat lids were used in the 1950's and 60's by a wide range of oil companies. Figure 12 shows a fully printed lid for which this style of lid was well suited.
Fig. 13, 14   Five section ring design used in the 1950's and 1960's by a large number of companies for lids (Fig.13), as well as for bottoms (Fig. 14).
Fig. 15   Outboard used this style of lid with a separate reusable cap that comes completely off the can and snaps back on. The example shown from Signal still has the protective seal that came on all full cans.

1960's and 70's

Fig. 16   Pull tab lids like this one as well as other different designs were primarily used on snowmobile and outboard cans in the 1960's and 70's

Fig. 17   Flat lid with raised center used during the 1960's and 1970's. Often used for cans with printed lids.

Fig.18, 19   Flat lid with a thin five section ring around the outside edge used on cans made in the 1970's.

1980's

Fig. 20   Flat lid with five section ring around the outside edge with a raised center.

Fig. 21   Flattened ring with raised center.

Examples of seams for use in dating quart oil cans

Fig. 22   Soldered seam without crimps was used on the earliest cans from the 1930's.

Fig. 23   Crimped soldered seam was common on cans from the late 1930's up until the 1950's.

Fig. 24   This soldered seam has an uncommon style of crimping and dates from the 1940's.

Fig. 25   This folded seam has crimping as well. This style of seam is unusual and rarely seen. Dates from the 1950's.

Fig. 26   Folded seam which replaced the crimped seam as the technology of choice in the 1950's and used until the 1980's. This seam was used until the advent of the composite can which has no seam.

Fig. 27   This is an example of some phrases that identify an oil can from the mid 1930's. The selling points of sealed quart cans were promoted with the phrases "Hermetically Sealed", "No Substitution", and "Full Measure" on the side of this can. The white vertical line to the left with arrows on both ends pointing to two circles has written inside the white line "Perfect circles at top and bottom guarantee contents have not been tampered with". Any can having these phrases or this line and circles combination is from the earliest period of sealed quart cans.

Fig. 16
#31 Amoco Snowmobile

Fig. 17
#325 Ford Premium

Fig. 22
#418 Hy Vis Premium

Fig. 23
#1168 Zephyr

Fig. 24
#183 Clark's Super

Fig. 18
#365 Golden Duron

Fig. 19
#381 Harley-Davidson Racing

Fig. 25
#207 Derby Penn Star

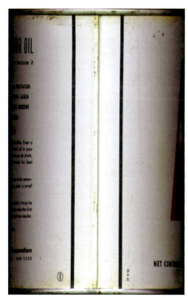
Fig. 26
#548 Macmillan Ring Free

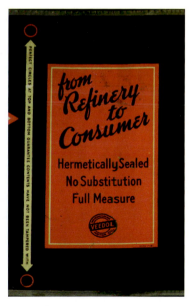
Fig. 27
Veedol (not pictured)

Fig. 20
#1121 Valvoline All Climate

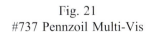
Fig. 21
#737 Pennzoil Multi-Vis

Before & After

These are just a few examples of how the actual oil cans appeared before being touched up on the computer. Most of the cans in this book had dents, scratches, rust, missing paint, missing text or graphics, and/or discolorations. Notice the Sooner Queen can which was misaligned when cut, causing the lettering on the bottom of the can to be cut off and a white border to appear at the top. The metallic cans were particularly difficult because of reflections. Even mint condition cans required touch up in order to eliminate the background. This process was very time consuming and required an eye for detail, an understanding of color, and a detailed knowledge and skill with the computer software.

 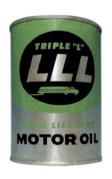  

KEY

Can material codes:

AL: aluminum
CP: composite
EP: embossed plastic
ERS: embossed ribbed steel (number suffix indicates the number of ribs in the can)
IRS: indented ribbed steel (number suffix indicates the number of ribs in the can)
PL: plastic
RS: ribbed steel
SS: straight steel

Color codes:

ALU:	aluminum	ORA:	orange
BLK:	black	PNK:	pink
BLU:	blue	PUR:	purple
BRN:	brown	RED:	red
CHR:	chrome	SIL:	silver
COP:	copper	STL:	steel
CRM:	cream	TAN:	tan
GLD:	gold	TUR:	turquoise
GRN:	green	WHT:	white
GRY:	gray	YEL:	yellow
MRN:	maroon		

A 4 and/or 5 to the right of the box below each picture indicates the can was also made in a round 4 and/or 5 quart size.

#	NAME	COMPANY	COLORS	MAT.	ERA	VALUE
1	Ace (w/ 25 cents price)	Ace of the Highway stations in and around Kansas City	Blu/Blu/Wht	SS	50's	$1000
2	Ace	G.W. Frogge Oil Co., Kansas City, Missouri	Blu/Wht	SS	50's	$750
3	Ace	Midwest Oil Co., Minneapolis, Fargo, Sioux Falls	Red/Blk/Wht	SS	50's	$25
4	Ace CX2	Midwest Oil Co., Minneapolis, Fargo, Sioux Falls	Red/Blk/Wht	SS	60's	$25
5	Ace High (with graphics)	Midwest Oil Co., Minneapolis, Fargo, Sioux Falls	Red/Blu/Wht	SS	40's	$250
6	Ace High (with black "High")	Midwest Oil Co., Minneapolis, Fargo, Sioux Falls	Red/Blk/Wht	SS	50's	$30
7	Ace High (with blue "High")	Midwest Oil Co., Minneapolis, Fargo, Sioux Falls	Red/Blk/Wht/Blu	SS	50's	$30
8	Ace Wil-Flo 5W-20	Midwest Oil Co., Minneapolis, Fargo, Sioux Falls	Blu/Wht/Blk/Red	SS	50's	$150
9	Ace Wil-Flo 10W-30	Midwest Oil Co., Minneapolis, Fargo, Sioux Falls	Blu/Wht/Blk/Red	SS	50's	$150
10	Actol	no company or address listed	Blu/Sil	SS	1953	$25
11	Actol	no company or address listed	Blu/Wht	SS	1954	$25
12	Admiral Penn	H.K. Stahl Co., St. Paul, Mn.	Grn/Wht/Red	SS	40's	$250
13	Aero Eastern	Christenson Oil Co., Portland, Ore.	Blk/Ora/Wht	SS	40's	$300
14	Aero	Christenson Oil Co., Portland, Ore.	Blk/Ora/Wht	SS	60's	$125
15	Allegany	Allegany Refiners Inc., Bolivar, N.Y.	Yel/Red	SS	30's	$85
16	AllPen Premium Crude	Bradford Oil Refining Co., Bradford, Penna.	Wht/Ora/Blu	SS	30's	$75
17	AllPen Refinery Sealed	Bradford Oil Refining Co., Bradford, Pa.	Blu/Ora/Wht	SS	30's	$100
18	All Purpose Hi-V.i.	Diamond Head Oil Refining Co. Inc., Kearny, N.J.	Stl/Ora/Grn	SS	50's	$20
19	All Purpose Hi-V.i.	Shur-Flo Oil Co., Inc., Kearny, N.J.	Stl/Ora/Grn	SS	60's	$20
20	All Purpose Hi-V.i.	Shur-Flo Oil Co., Inc., Kearny, N.J.	Wht/Ora/Grn	SS	50's	$20
21	Alubco Heavy Duty	American Lubricants Co., Dayton 1, Ohio	Wht/Blu/Red	SS	50's	$275
22	Alubco Ultra-V	no company listed	Red/Wht/Blu	SS	60's	$40
23	American	American Oil Co.	Red/Wht	SS	60's	$25
24	American HD-M (w/o contents and address)	American Oil Co., Chicago, Il.	Wht/Blu/Red	SS	1-61	$15
25	American HD-M (with contents and address)	American Oil Co., Chicago, Il.	Wht/Blu/Red	CP	60's	$8
26	American S-1	American Oil Co., Chicago, Il.	Wht/Blu/Red	SS	1-61	$15
27	American S-3	American Oil Co., Chicago, Il.	Wht/Blu/Red	SS	1-61	$15
28	American Truck and Bus	American Oil Co., Chicago, Il.	Wht/Blu/Red	CP	11-61	$20

ALL PRICES LISTED IN THIS BOOK ARE FOR GRADE 9 CANS

3-9 Ace to Ace Wil-Flo 10W-30: See also 584-587 Midwest, 643 MOCO, 1155 Wil-Flo

10,11 Actol was a discount brand sold by Esso. See also 171 Challenge, 238-292 Esso, 667 Oilex to 670 Oklahoma Heavy Duty, 672 Palubco, 684 Pate Valve Glide, 1072-1076 Uniflo

12 Admiral Penn: See also 99 Arctic Blue Snowmobile Oil, 294 Exceloyl, 878 Servoil #2, 1065-1069 Trophy

13,14 Aero Eastern: See also 864 Real Penn

16,17 Allpen: See also 457 K-24

18 All Purpose: See also 225 Diamond Outboard and 2 Cycle, 662 Neptune

18-20 All Purpose: Can 18 is produced by a different company than cans 19 and 20 despite having the same design.

23-28 American to American Truck and Bus: See also 29 American Outbaord to 78 Amoco Ultimate, 673 Pan-Am Permalube Heavy Duty, 674, 675 Panoco

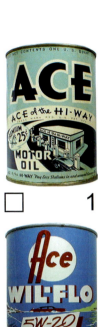 1
 2
 3
 4
 5
 6
 7
 8
 9
 10
 11
 12
 13
 14
 15
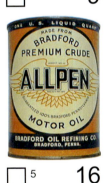 16
 17
 18
 19
 20
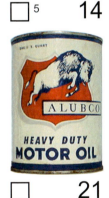 21
 22
 23
 24
 25
 26
 27
 28

#	NAME	COMPANY	COLORS	MAT.	ERA	VALUE
29	American Outboard	American Oil Co., Chicago, Il.	Red/Wht/Blu	CP	10-64	$20
30	American Snowmobile	American Oil Co., Chicago Il. 60680	Wht/Blu/Red	CP	9-68	$15
31	Amoco American Snowmobile	American Oil Co., Chicago Il. 60680	Wht/Chr/Blu/Red	SS	8-72	$10
32	AMO Anti-freeze	American Oil Co., Baltimore, Md., New York, N.Y.	Wht/Blu/Red/Blk	SS	40's	$65
33	Amoco Super Anti-freeze	American Oil Co.	Blu/Wht/Ora/Blk	SS	50's	$65
34	Amoco	American Oil Co.	Grn/Red/Wht/Blk	SS	50's	$20
35	Amoco	American Oil Co.	Wht/Blu/Red/Blk	SS	50's	$15
36	Amoco (torch logo)	American Oil Co.	Wht/Blu/Red	SS	60's	$15
37	Penn-Amo	American Oil Co.	Sil/Red/Blu	SS	30's	$85
38	Amoco Penn	American Oil Co.	Sil/Blu/Chr/Red	SS	50's	$20
39	Amoco Penn (torch logo)	American Oil Co.	Sil/Blu/Chr/Red	SS	50's	$20
40	Amoco Permalube (Permalube Processed)	American Oil Co.	Wht/Red/Blu/Blk	SS	40's	$50
41	Amoco Permalube	American Oil Co.	Wht/Blu/Red/Blk	SS	50's	$15
42	American Permalube	American Oil Co., Chicago, Il.	Wht/Blu/Red	SS	1-61	$15
43	Permalube (with "Amoco" in torch logo)	No company or location	Wht/Blu/Red	SS	60's	$35
44	American Permalube (Net Contents 1 US Qt.)	American Oil Co., Chicago, Il.	Wht/Blu/Red	CP	8-64	$10
45	Amoco Super Permalube	American Oil Co.	Wht/Gld/Blu/Red	SS	50's	$20
46	American Super Permalube	American Oil Co., Chicago, Il.	Wht/Gld/Blu/Red	SS	1-61	$15
47	American Super Permalube	American Oil Co., Chicago, Il.	Wht/Gld/Blu/Red	CP	11-61	$10
48	American Super Premium LDO	American Oil Co., Chicago, Il.	Wht/Gld/Red/Blu	CP	7-62	$35
49	Artex	American Oil Co., Chicago, Il.	Red/Wht/Blu	SS	1-61	$15
50	Amolube	American Oil Co., Chicago, Il.	Wht/Red/Blu	SS	4-61	$15
51	Amolube	American Oil Co., Chicago, Il.	Wht/Red/Blu	CP	11-61	$10
52	Amolube (with "Amoco" in torch logo)	No company or location	Red/Blu	SS	60's	$35
53	Amolube	American Oil Co., Chicago, Il.	Red/Wht/Blu	CP	0 66	$0
54	Amoco Dexron A-1-F	Amoco Oil Co., Chicago, Il. 60680	Wht/Blu/Red	CP	9-67	$10
55	Permalube	American Oil Co., Chicago, Il.	Blu/Wht/Sil/Red	CP	9-66	$8
56	Super Permalube	American Oil Co., Chicago, Il.	Gld/Wht/Blu/Red	CP	9-66	$8

ALL PRICES LISTED IN THIS BOOK ARE FOR GRADE 9 CANS

29-56   American Outboard - Super Permalube: See also 23 American to 28 American Truck and Bus, 57-78 Amoco, 673 Pan-Am Permalube Heavy Duty, 674, 675 Panoco
42   American Permalube: A composite variation exists dated 1-61
43,52   These cans are believed to be for export only.
46,47   American Super Permalube: These two cans are very similar. The word "Super" on 47 is farther from the top edge and uses thinner letters.

☐ 29

☐ 30

☐ 31

☐ 32

☐ 33

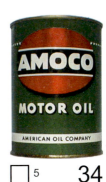
☐5 34

☐5 35

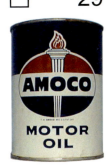
☐5 36

☐5 37

☐5 38

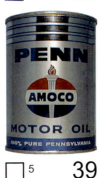
☐5 39

☐5 40

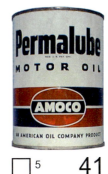
☐5 41

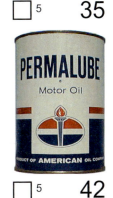
☐5 42

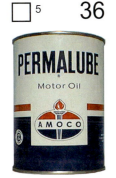
☐ 43

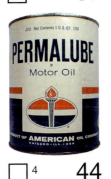
☐4 44

☐5 45

☐ 46

☐ 47

☐4 48

☐ 49

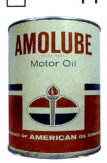
☐ 50

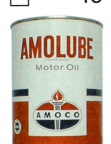
☐ 51

☐ 52

☐ 53

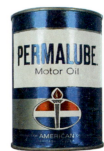
☐ 54

☐ 55

☐ 56

#	NAME	COMPANY	COLORS	MAT.	ERA	VALUE
57	Amoco M-V	American Oil Co., Chicago, Il.	Wht/Chr/Red/Blu	CP	5-66	$8
58	Amoco 100	American Oil Co., Chicago, Il.	Wht/Red/Blu	CP	5-66	$8
59	Amoco 200	American Oil Co., Chicago, Il.	Wht/Blu/Red	CP	5-66	$8
60	Amolube	Amoco Oil Co., Chicago, Il. 60680	Red/Wht	CP	1-73	$4
61	Amoco Permalube	Amoco Oil Co., Chicago, Il. 60680	Blu/Wht	CP	4-72	$4
62	Amoco 200	Amoco Oil Co., Chicago, Il. 60680	Wht/Blu	CP	1-73	$4
63	Amoco 300	Amoco Oil Co., Chicago, Il. 60680	Wht/Ora/Chr	CP	1-77	$4
64	Amoco ATF Type F	Amoco Oil Co., Chicago, Il. 60680	Wht/Red	CP	9-82	$3
65	Amoco Dexron-II ATF	Amoco Oil Co., Chicago Ill. 60680	Wht/Blu/Red	CP	9-82	$3
66	Amoco 200 Heavy Duty	Amoco Oil Co., Chicago, Il. 60680	Blu/Wht	CP	9-82	$3
67	Amoco Permalube	Amoco Oil Co., Chicago, Il. 60680	Blu/Wht	CP	3-78	$3
68	Amoco Amolube	Amoco Oil Co., Chicago, Il. 60680	Red/Wht	CP	3-78	$3
69	Amoco LDO Super Permalube	Amoco Oil Co., Chicago, Il. 60680	Gld.Blu/Red	CP	1-73	$4
70	Amoco LDO All Weather 10W-40	Amoco Oil Co., Chicago, Il. 60680	Gld/Blu	CP	1-80	$3
71	Amoco M-V All Season 10W-30	Amoco Oil Co., Chicago, Il. 60680	Sil/Blu	CP	1-80	$3
72	Amoco Super Permalube	Amoco Oil Co., Chicago, Il. 60680	Sil/Blu	CP	1-73	$3
73	Amoco ATF Type F	Amoco Oil Co., Chicago, Il. 60680	Grn/Blk/Wht	CP	2-85	$3
74	Amoco 200 Gas or Diesel Heavy Duty	Amoco Oil Co., Chicago, Il. 60680	Ora/Blk/Wht	CP	9-84	$3
75	Amoco 300 Super Duty	Amoco Oil Co., Chicago, Il. 60680	Ora/Blk/Wht	CP	9-84	$3
76	Amoco LDO 10W-30	Amoco Oil Co., Chicago, Il. 60680	Sil/Blk/Wht	CP	9-84	$3
77	Amoco LDO 10W-40	Amoco Oil Co., Chicago, Il. 60680	Gld/Blk/Wht	CP	9-84	$3
78	Amoco Ultimate	Amoco Oil Co., Chicago, Il. 60680	Blk/Wht/Blu/Red	CP	2-82	$3
79	Anchor	Anchor Petroleum Co., Corpus Christi, Tx.	Grn/Crm/Red	SS	30's	$90
80	Anchor Heavy Duty	Anchor Oil Corp., Omaha, Neb.	Blu/Wht/Ora	SS	40's	$75
81	Anchor Precision Built	Anchor Oil Corp., Omaha, Neb.	Ora/Wht/Blu	SS	50's	$65
82	Antioarbo	Cincinnati Oil Works, Cincinnati, Oh.	Yel/Ora/Blk/Wht	SS	40's	$100
83	A P Type A ATF (white stripe on top)	Action Industries, P.O.B. 5146, Kansas City, Ks.	Red/Wht	CP	60's	$3
84	A P Type A ATF (white stripe on bottom)	Inter-state Oil Co., Inc., 57 Shawnee Ave., Kansas City, Ks. 66119	Red/Wht	CP	70's	$3

ALL PRICES LISTED IN THIS BOOK ARE FOR GRADE 9 CANS

57-78   Amoco M-V to Amoco Ultimate: See also 23 American to 28 American Truck and Bus, 29 American Outboard to 56 Super Permalube, 673 Pan-Am Permalube Heavy Duty, 674, 675 Panoco

83,84   AP Type A ATF: These two cans are produced by different companies despite having a similar appearance.

84   AP Type A ATF: See also 435-447 Interstate, 660, 661 National Special

#	NAME	COMPANY	COLORS	MAT.	ERA	VALUE
85	APCO 10W-30	Apco Oil Corp., Oklahoma City	Wht/Gld/Red	SS	50's	$60
86	APCO X-S Heavy Duty	Anderson-Prichard Oil Corp. Oklahoma City	Wht/Red	AL	60's	$45
87	APCO X-S Extra Heavy Duty	Apco Oil Corp., Oklahoma City	Wht/Red/Sil	CP	60's	$12
88	APCO 10W-40	Apco Oil Corp., Oklahoma City, Ok. 73102	Gld/Blu/Wht/Red	SS	70's	$40
89	APCO 10W-40 Long Distance	Apco Oil Corp., Oklahoma City, Ok.	Gld/Blu/Wht/Red	SS	70's	$45
90	APCO Defiance Non-Detergent	Apco Oil Corp., Oklahoma City, Ok.	Red/Wht/Blu	CP	70's	$10
91	APCO Super 3	APCO Oil Corp., Oklahoma City, Okla. 73102	Grn/Wht/Sil/Blu	CP	70's	$10
92	APCO X-S Extra Heavy Duty	Apco Oil Corp., Oklahoma City, Ok.	Blu/Wht/Red/Sil	CP	70's	$10
93	Apex Non-Detergent ("Apex" in red)	Denver Oil Co., Oklahoma City, Ok. 73109	Wht/Red/Yel	CP	70's	$4
94	Apex Non-Detergent ("Apex" in black)	Denver Oil Co., Oklahoma City, Ok. 73143	Wht/Blk/Yel	CP	80's	$4
95	Approved ATF Type A Suffix A	Industrial Lubricants Company Inc., San Antonio 8, Tx.	Wht/Gld/Blu/Sil	CP	60's	$4
96	Approved ATF	Industrial Lubricants Co., San Antonio, Tx. 78220	Wht/Gld/Blu/Sil	CP	80's	$4
97	APR Super Duty Plus	American Petroleum Resources, Santa Fe Springs, Cal. 90670	Red/Wht/Gld	CP	80's	$10
98	Aptol	Rushing Oil Co., Eldorado, Ark.	Wht/Blu/Red	SS	40's	$35
99	Arctic Blue Heavy Duty Snowmobile Oil	Metalcote Grease & Oil Co., St Paul, Minn. 55102	Blu/Wht/Gld	CP	70's	$15
100	Armor Heavy Duty for MS-DG	Petroleum Chemicals Co., Danville, Il. & Los Angeles, Ca.	Wht/Red/Blu	SS	60's	$75
101	Artic Flo- Methanol Anti-freeze	Petroleum Chemicals Co., Danville Il.	Tur/Red/Wht	SS	50's	$30
102	ATF Automatic Transmission Fluid	Warren Oil Co., Omaha, Neb. 68102	Wht/Red	CP	70's	$3
103	Barnsdall Stabilized	(no company or address listed)	Red/Wht/Blu	SS	30's	$100
104	Barnsdall 100% Pure Pennsylvania	Barnsdall Refining Corporation	Grn/Wht/Blk/Red	SS	30's	$100
105	Be Square	Bareco Oil Co.	Wht/Blu/Red	SS	40's	$150
106	B (inside square) Supreme	Bareco Oil Co.	Wht/Blu/Red	SS	40's	$125
107	Beaver-Penn	Freedom Oil Co., Freedom, Pa.	Yel/Blu/Wht	SS	1936	$350
108	Beeline Heavy Duty	Western States Refining Co., North Salt Lake, Utah	Blk/Yel/Red	SS	60's	$500
109	Beeline Ultra Lube (reverse of 349)	Frontier Refining Co., Denver, Co.	Red/Wht/Gld/Blk	CP	60's	$50
110	Bellube	The Bell Oil and Gas Co., Grandfield and Tuksa Ok.	Ora/Blu/Wht	SS	30's	$450
111	Ben Hur	Ben Hur Oil Co., Los Angeles-New Orleans	Red/Wht/Blk	SS	60's	$225
112	Best Premium 35 cents	Waggoner & Chadil, Los Angeles, Ca.	Wht/Red/Blu	SS	40's	$50

ALL PRICES LISTED IN THIS BOOK ARE FOR GRADE 9 CANS

85-92 APCO 10W-30 to APCO X-S Extra Heavy Duty: See also 172 Challenge Super Refined, 173 Challenge X-S, 203 Defiance
95,96 Approved ATF: See also 316 5 Star, 370, 371 Golden State
99 Arctic Blue Heavy Duty Snowmobile Oil: See also 12 Admiral Penn, 294 Exceloyl, 878 Servoil #2, 1065-1069 Trophy
100,101 Armor Heavy Duty, Artic Flo: See also 115 Blue Star Anti-freeze, 838, 839 Protecto, 1149 Weather-Mate
102 ATF Automatic Transmission Fluid: See also 360-362 Gold Bond, 531 Life, 823 Polar Anti-freeze
103-106 Barnsdall Stabilized to B (inside square) Supreme: See also 645, 646 Monamotor, 974 Superoil, 1135 Victory
107 Beaver Penn: See also 337 Fort Pitt, 339-341 Freedom, 350-352 Galena, 1054 Tip Top Penn, 1100-1134 Valvoline
108,109 Beeline Heavy Duty, Beeline Ultra Lube: See also 342-349 Frontier

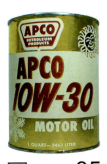 85
 86
 87
 88
 89
 90
 91

 92
 93
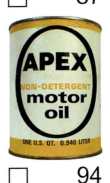 94
 95
 96
 97
 98

 99
 ⁵ 100
 101
 102
 ⁵ 103
 ⁵ 104
 105

 106
 ⁵ 107
 108
 109
 110
 111
 112

#	NAME	COMPANY	COLORS	MAT.	ERA	VALUE
113	Blue Bonnet Economical	no company or location listed	Blu/Wht	SS	40's	$275
114	Blue Bonnet Parrafin Base	no company or location listed	Blu/Wht	SS	40's	$275
115	Blue Star Methanol Anti-freeze	Petroleum Chemicals Co., Danville, Il.	Chr/Blu/Red	SS	50's	$20
116	Blue Streak	Browder Oil Co., Fort Worth, Texas	Yel/Blu	SS	40's	$65
117	Boron All Season 10W30	Boron Oil, Division BP Oil Inc., Cleveland, Ohio 44115	Sil/Blk/Chr/Blu	CP	80's	$8
118	Browder 76	Browder Oil Co., Fort Worth, Texas	Blu/Yel	SS	40's	$75
119	Browder 76	Browder Oil Co., Fort Worth, Texas	Yel/Blu/Red	SS	50's	$50
120	Browder 76	Browder Distributing Co., Fort Worth, Tx. 76106	Yel/Blu/Red	CP	60's	$15
121	Buick Special for Automatic Transmissions	Buick Motor Division, General Motors Corp.	Blu/Wht/Blk	SS	50's	$60
122	Buick Special Buick Oil for Dynaflow Drive	Buick Motor Division, General Motors Corp.	Blu/Wht/Blk	SS	50's	$60
123	Buick Special Buick Rear Axle Lubricant	Buick Motor Division, General Motors Corp.	Blu/Wht/Blk	SS	50's	$60
124	Buick Methanol Anti-Freeze	Buick Motor Division, General Motors Corp., Flint, Mich.	Blu/Wht/Red/Blk	SS	50's	$60
125	Buick Non Evaporating Anti-Freeze	Buick Motor Division, General Motors Corp., Flint, Mich.	Blu/Wht/Red/Gry	SS	50's	$85
126	Bustrux Homogenized HD	Warren Refining & Chemical Co., Cleveland	Ora/Blk/Wht	SS	40's	$45
127	Bustrux	Warren Refining & Chemical Co., Cleveland, Oh.	Ora/Blk	SS	60's	$30
128	Cactus Super Duty	Southwestern Petroleum Co., (no location given)	Blk/Grn/Yel	SS	50's	$350
129	C.A.M. Castor Additive Motorcycle	Indian, Springfield, Mass.	Grn/Wht/Red	SS	50's	$225
130	Case New Hi-Lo TCH Oil	J.I. Case Co., Racine Wis.	Wht/Chr/Blk	SS	1-60	$15
131	Case Engine Gard Extra Heavy Duty	J.I. Case, A Tenneco Co., 700 State St., Racine, Wi. 53404	Wht/Blk/Ora	CP	80's	$4
132	Case HDM Oil MS 1103	J.I. Case, A Tenneco Co., Racine, Wi.	Wht/Blk/Ora	CP	80's	$4
133	Case HDM Oil JIC 125	J.I. Case, A Tenneco Co., Racine, Wi. 53404	Wht/Ora/Blk	CP	80's	$4
134	Case I.H. Low Ash SAE 30	J.I. Case, A Tenneco Co., Racine, Wi.	Wht/Blk/Gry/Red	CP	80's	$4
135	Case I.H. No. 1 Multi-Viscosity	J.I. Case, A Tenneco Co., Racine, Wi. 53404	Wht/Yel/Blk/Gry	CP	80's	$4
136	Case I.H. No. 1 SAE 30	J.I. Case, A Tenneco Co., Racine, Wi. 53404	Wht/Yel/Blk/Gry	CP	80's	$4
137	Castrol (with script "Castrol")	C.C. Wakefield & Co. Limited, London and N.Y.	Grn/Wht/Blk/Red	SS	40's	$50
138	Castrol (with "Castrol" logo angled)	Castrol Oils Inc., Newark, N.J./San Francisco	Grn/Wht/Red	SS	60's	$20
139	Castrol (with "wakefield")	Castrol Oils Inc., Newark, N.J.	Grn/Wht/Red	SS	60's	$20
140	Castrol (with "Castrol" logo straight)	Castrol Oils Inc., Newark, N.J. 07105	Grn/Wht/Red	CP	70's	$6

ALL PRICES LISTED IN THIS BOOK ARE FOR GRADE 9 CANS

115   Blue Star Anti-freeze: See also 100 Armor, 101 Artic Flo Anti-freeze, 838, 839 Protecto, 1149 Weather Mate
116   Blue Streak: See also 118-120 Browder 76
117   Boron was the brandname used by Sohio for marketing outside of Ohio. See also 170 Cetron HD, 181 CHD, 298, 299 Facto, 365 Golden Duron, 659 Multron, 663, 664 Nitrex, 665 Nitron, 666 Octron, 829-833 Premex, 862, 863 QVO, 895 Sixty Two, 897-917 Sohio
118-120 Browder: See also 116 Blue Streak
129   C.A.M.: See also 430-433 Indian
130-136 Case New Hi-Lo TCH Oil to Case IH No. 1 SAE 30: See also 421-426 IH

 113
 114
 115
 116
 117
 118
 119
 120
 121
 122
 123
 124
 125
 126
 127
 128
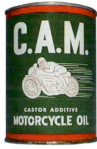 129
 130
 131
 132
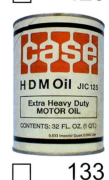 133

 134
 135
 136
 137
 138
 139
140

#	NAME	COMPANY	COLORS	MAT.	ERA	VALUE
141	Castrol Outboard (with screw lid)	C.C. Wakefield and Co. Ltd., London and New York	Grn/Wht/Red	SS	50's	$85
142	Castrol Outboard ("Castrol" in script)	C.C. Wakefield and Co. Ltd., London and New York	Wht/Grn/Red/Blk	SS	60's	$40
143	Castrol Outboard ("Castrol" not in script)	C.C. Wakefield and Co. Ltd., London and New York	Wht/Grn/Red/Blk	SS	60's	$35
144	Castrol SAE 10W/30 Heavy Duty	Castrol Oils, Inc., Newark, N.J./SanFrancisco	Wht/Red/Grn	SS	50's	$30
145	Castrol Nanouk Anti-freeze	C.C. Wakefield and Co. Ltd., London and New York	Wht/Grn/Red	SS	60's	$60
146	Castrol Racing	Castrol Oils Inc., Newark, N.J./San Francisco	Wht/Grn/Red	SS	60's	$45
147	Castrol Racing (w/address & contents text)	Castrol Oils Inc., Newark, N.J.	Wht/Grn/Red	SS	60's	$45
148	Castrol Racing	Castrol Oils Inc., Newark, N.J. 07105	Grn/Wht/Ora	SS	70's	$35
149	Castrol GP Racing	Castrol Oils Inc., Newark, N.J. 07105	Ora/Grn/Wht/Blk	CP	70's	$10
150	Castrol XLR Racing Oil	Castrol Oils Inc., Newark, N.J. 07105	Wht/Red/Grn/Blk	CP	70's	$10
151	Castrol GTX High Performance Motor Oil	Burmah-Castrol Inc.,Hackensack N.J. 07601	Wht/Ora/Grn/Blk	CP	80's	$4
152	Castrol GTX Super Multi Grade	Burmah-Castrol Inc.,Hackensack N.J. 07601	Wht/Ora/Grn/Blk	CP	80's	$4
153	Castrol GTX Super Multi Grade "Engineered...	Burmah-Castrol Inc.,Hackensack N.J. 07601	Wht/Ora/Grn/Blk	CP	80's	$4
154	Castrol GTX Super Multi Grade 10W/40	Burmah-Castrol Inc.,Hackensack N.J. 07601	Wht/Ora/Grn/Blk	CP	80's	$4
155	Castrol GTX Super Multi Grade 20W/50	Burmah-Castrol Inc.,Hackensack N.J. 07601	Wht/Ora/Grn/Blk	CP	80's	$4
156	Castrol GTX Super Multi.. Turbo Approved	Burmah-Castrol Inc.,Hackensack N.J. 07601	Wht/Ora/Grn/Blk	CP	80's	$4
157	Castrol High Performance Snowmobile	Castrol Oils Inc., Newark, N.J. 07105	Blu/Wht/Red	CP	70's	$10
158	Castrol High Performance Snowmobile	Burmah-Castrol Inc., Hackensack N.J. 07601	Wht/Blu/Red	CP	80's	$8
159	Castrol Heavy Duty	Castrol Oils Inc., Newark, N.J. 07105	Grn/Wht/Ora	CP	80's	$4
160	Castrol Heavy Duty	Burmah-Castrol Inc., Hackensack N.J. 07601	Wht/GrnOra/Blk	CP	80's	$4
161	Castrol Multi-Grade	Burmah-Castrol Inc., Hackensack, N.J.	Wht/Ora/Grn/Blk	CP	80's	$4
162	Castrol Grand Prix	Castrol Oils Inc., Newark, N.J. 07105	Grn/Wht/Red	CP	70's	$8
163	Castrol Grand Prix Two Cycle	Castrol Oils Inc., Newark, N.J. 07105	Grn/Wht/Red	CP	70's	$8
164	Castrol Grand Prix 2 Stroke SAE 30	Burmah-Castrol Inc., Hackensack, N.J. 07601	Grn/Wht/Red/Blk	CP	80's	$8
165	Castrol Grand Prix 4 Stroke	Burmah-Castrol Inc., Hackensack, N.J. 07601	Grn/Wht/Red/Blk	CP	80's	$8
166	Castrol S Super 4 Stroke	Burmah-Castrol Inc., Hackensack, N.J.	Chr/Blk/Ora	CP	80's	$8
167	Castrol XL 20W-40	Castrol Oils Inc., Newark, N.J. 07105	Wht/Grn/Red	CP	80's	$5
168	Castrolite Multigrade SAE 10W-20W-30	Castrol Oils Inc., Newark, N.J. 07105	Wht/Grn/Ora	CP	80's	$5

ALL PRICES LISTED IN THIS BOOK ARE FOR GRADE 9 CANS

 ☐ 141
 ☐ 142
 ☐ 143
 ☐ 144
 ☐ 145
 ☐ 146
 ☐ 147

 ☐ 148
 ☐ 149
 ☐ 150
 ☐ 151
 ☐ 152
 ☐ 153
 ☐ 154

 ☐ 155
 ☐ 156
 ☐ 157
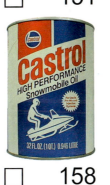 ☐ 158
 ☐ 159
 ☐ 160
 ☐ 161

 ☐ 162 ☐ 163
 ☐ 164
 ☐ 165
 ☐ 166
 ☐ 167
 ☐ 168

#	NAME	COMPANY	COLORS	MAT.	ERA	VALUE
169	Certified Penn	Certified Service Stations, Muncie, Ind.	Blu/Red/Wht	SS	50's	$750
170	Cetron HD	Boron Oil Co., Cleveland, Oh. 44115 (on bottom lid)	Wht/Red/Blu/Gld	SS	70's	$30
171	Challenge	Pate Oil Co., Milwaukee, Wis.	Wht/Blu/Red	SS	1954	$125
172	Challenge Super Refined	Anderson-Prichard Oil Corp., Okla. City, Ok.	Blu/Wht/Red	SS	40's	$75
173	Challenge X S	Anderson-Prichard Oil Corp., Okla. City, Ok.	Wht/Blu/Red	SS	40's	$50
174	Champion Non Detergent	Lowe Oil Co., Clinton, Mo.	Ora/Blk/Wht	SS	60's	$20
175	Champion ("Two Cycle" on lid)	Lowe Oil Co., Clinton, Mo.	Ora/Blk/Wht	CP	60's	$6
176	Champion (with 1 US Quart)	Lowe Oil Co., Clinton, Mo. 64735	Blk/Red/Wht/Sil	CP	70's	$4
177	Champion (with 1 Quart(32 FL. OZ.))	Lowe Oil Co., Clinton, Mo. 64735	Blk/Red/Wht/Sil	CP	80's	$4
178	Champion (green)	Lowe Oil Co., Clinton, Mo. 64735	Grn/Red/Wht	CP	70's	$4
179	Champion ATF	Lowe Oil Co., Clinton, Mo. 64735	Grn/Ora/Wht	CP	70's	$5
180	Champion ATF	Lowe Oil Co., Clinton, Mo. 64735	Ora/Wht/Blk	CP	70's	$5
181	CHD	Baron Oil Co., Cleveland, Oh. 44115	Wht/Blu/Red/Gld	SS	65-66	$30
182	Clark Permanent Anti-freeze	Clark Oil & Refining Corp., Milwaukee, Wis.	Wht/Org/Blk	SS	40's	$85
183	Clark's Super	Clarks Super Products, Milwaukee	Wht/Ora/Grn	SS	40's	$125
184	Clark's Super Penn	Clark's Super Gas Co., Milwaukee, Wis.	Ora/Wht/Grn	SS	40's	$175
185	Clark Premium Petco-lube	Clark Oil and Refining Corp.	Ora/Wht/Grn	SS	50's	$85
186	Clark 10W-30 Special H.D.	Clark Oil and Refining Corp.	Gld/Wht/Red	SS	50's	$85
187	Clark Permanent Anti-freeze Summer Coolant	Clark Oil & Refining Corp., 8530 W. National, Milwaukee, Wis. 53227	Blu/Wht/Ora	SS	60's	$75
188	Clark Permanent Anti-freeze	Clark Oil & Refining Corp., 8530 W. National, Milwaukee, Wis. 53227	Blu/Wht/Ora	SS	60's	$75
189	Clark 10W-30	Clark Oil & Refining Corp., Milwaukee, Wis. 53227	Wht/Ora/Blk	CP	80's	$15
190	Clark 10W-40	Clark Oil & Refining Corp., Milwaukee, Wis. 53227	Wht/Pur/Ora/Blk	CP	80's	$15
191	Clark 100	Clark Oil and Refining Corp.	Wht/Chr/Ora/Blk	SS	60's	$45
192	Clark 100	Clark Oil & Refining Corp., Milwaukee, Wis. 53227	Wht/Sil/Ora/Blk	SS	60's	$45
193	Clark 100	Clark Oil & Refining Corp., Milwaukee, Wis.	Wht/Sil/Ora/Blk	CP	80's	$15
194	Clark Super (with "ONE U.S. QUART" on side)	Clark Oil and Refining Corp.	Wht/Blk/Ora	SS	60's	$35
195	Clark Super (with "ONE U.S. QUART.")	Clark Oil and Refining Corp.	Wht/Blk/Ora	SS	60's	$35
196	Clark Super (with "NET 1 U.S. QUART.")	Clark Oil & Refining Corp., Milwaukee, Wis. 53227	Wht/Blk/Ora	SS	60's	$35

ALL PRICES LISTED IN THIS BOOK ARE FOR GRADE 9 CANS

170,181 Cetron HD & CHD: See also 117 Boron, 298, 299 Facto, 365 Golden Duron, 659 Multron, 663, 664 Nitrex, 665 Nitron, 666 Octron, 829-833 Premex, 862, 863 QVO, 895 Sixty Two, 897-917 Sohio

171 Challenge: Pate Oil Co. became part of Esso. See also 10,11 Actol, 238-292 Esso, 667 Oilex to 670 Oklahoma Heavy Duty, 672 Palubco, 684 Pate Valve Glide, 1072-1076 Uniflo

172,173 Challenge Super Refined, Challenge XS: See also 85-92 APCO, 203 Defiance

174-180 Champion Non Detergent to Champion ATF: See also 296, 297 Extra Lube

 169
 170
 171
 172
 173
 174
 175

 176
 177
 178
 179
 180
 181
 182

 183
 184
 185
 186
 187
 188
 189

 190
 191
 192
 193
 194
 195
 196

#	NAME	COMPANY	COLORS	MAT.	ERA	VALUE
197	Comet Lube	Tresler Oil Co., Cincinnati, Oh.	Red/Wht/Blu	CP	60's	$35
198	Convoy "The Energy Saving Oil"	Conklin Company Inc., Shakopee, Mn. 55379	Blk/Wht/Red/Gld	CP	80's	$4
199	Convoy "The 25,000 mile Oil"	Conklin Company Inc., Shakopee, Mn. 55379	Blk/Wht/Red/Gld	CP	80's	$4
200	Coreco (with "Coreco" in map)	Continental Refining Co., Oil City, Pa.	Wht/Red/Blk	SS	30's	$75
201	Coreco (w/"Quality" inside oval)	Continental Refining Co., Oil City, Pa.	Yel/Blk/Red	SS	40's	$60
202	Coreco Penn	Continental Refining Co., Oil City, Pa.	Yel/Blk/Red	SS	40's	$60
203	Defiance	Anderson Prichard, Oklahoma City, Ok.	Wht/Blu/Red	SS	50's	$300
204	Derby Penn Star (with DOCo logo)	Derby Products, Wichita, Ks.	Wht/Blu/Red	SS	30's	$300
205	Derby Triumph (with DOCo logo)	Derby Oil Co., Wichita, Ks.	Red/Wht/Blu	SS	30's	$300
206	Derby Vitalized (with DOCo logo)	Derby Oil Co., Wichita, Ks.	Red/Wht/Blu	SS	30's	$250
207	Derby Penn Star (w/large "Penn Star")	Derby Oil Co., Wichita, Ks.	Blu/Wht/Red	SS	50's	$75
208	Derby Triumph (w/large "Triumph")	Derby Oil Co., Wichita, Ks.	Red/Wht/Blu	SS	50's	$75
209	Derby Vitalized (w/large "Vitalized")	Derby Oil Co., Wichita, Ks.	Wht/Red/Blu	SS	50's	$75
210	Derby Flex-Lube (w/o stars)	Derby Refining Co., Wichita, Ks.	Wht/Red/Blu	SS	50's	$40
211	Derby Flex-Lube (w/twinkling stars)	Derby Refining Co., Div. of Colo. Oil & Gas Corp.	Blu/Wht/Red	SS	60's	$40
212	Derby Improved Star-Trans ATF	Derby Refining Co., Div. of Colo. Oil & Gas Corp., Wichita, Ks.	Yel/Wht/Red/Blu	SS	50's	$40
213	Derby Super-X Flex-Lube (w/twinkling stars)	Derby Refining Co., Div. of Colo. Oil & Gas Corp.	Wht/Gld/Red/Blu	AL	60's	$35
214	Derby Triumph (w/twinkling stars)	Derby Refining Co., Div. of Colo. Oil & Gas Corp.	Red/Wht/Blu	SS	60's	$50
215	Derby Permanent Anti-Freeze	Derby Refining Co., Div. of Colo. Oil & Gas	Wht/Red/Gld/Blu	SS	60's	$30
216	Derby Star-Trans Fluid	Derby Refining Co., Wichita, Ks. 67201	Blu/Red/Chr/Wht	CP	70's	$7
217	Derby Super-Flex	Derby Refining Co., Wichita, Ks. 67201	Wht/Blu/Gld/Red	CP	70's	$7
218	Derby 10W-30	Derby Refining Co., Div. of Colo. Oil & Gas Corp, Wichita, Ks.	Wht/Red/Gld/Blu	CP	70's	$7
219	Derby Triumph	Derby Refining Co., Div. of Colo. Oil & Gas Corp., Wichita, Ks. 67201	Wht/Red/Chr/Blu	CP	70's	$7
220	Derby All Season Ultra Life 10W-40	Derby Refining Co., Wichita, Ks. 67201	Blu/Gld/Wht/Red	CP	80's	$5
221	Dezol "Oiloy"	Universal Motor Oils Co., Wichita, Ks.	Cop/Blk/Wht	SS	40's	$25
222	Dezol "Oiloy"	Universal Motor Oils Co., Wichita, Ks.	Gld/Blu	SS	60's	$15
223	Dezol "Oiloy"	Universal Motor Oils Co., Wichita, Ks.	Gld/Blu	RS	70's	$15
224	Dezol	Universal Motor Oils Co. Inc., P.O. Box 11145, Wichita, Ks. 67202	Brn/Wht/Blk	CP	80's	$4

ALL PRICES LISTED IN THIS BOOK ARE FOR GRADE 9 CANS

203   Defiance: See also 85-92 APCO, 172 Challenge Super Refined, 173 Challenge XS

221-224 Dezol: See also 458-461 Kan-O-Gold, 876 Ser-Vis, 1083-1099 Universal

☐ 197 ☐ 198 ☐ 199 ☐ 200 ☐ 201 ☐5 202 ☐ 203

   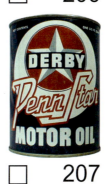   

☐5 204 ☐ 205 ☐ 206 ☐ 207 ☐ 208 ☐ 209 ☐ 210

 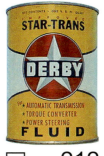     

☐ 211 ☐ 212 ☐ 213 ☐ 214 ☐ 215 ☐ 216 ☐ 217

 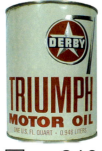     

☐ 218 ☐ 219 ☐ 220 ☐ 221 ☐ 222 ☐ 223 ☐ 224

#	NAME	COMPANY	COLORS	MAT.	ERA	VALUE
225	Diamond Outboard and 2 Cycle	Diamond Head Oil Refining Co., Inc., Kearny, N.J.	Wht/Grn/Blk	SS	50's	$125
226	Dura	Westland Oil Co., Minot, N.D.	Grn/Blk/Wht	SS	30's	$85
227	Dura Superior (Dura in red script)	Westland Oil Co., Minot, N.D.	Wht/Grn/Red/Blk	SS	40's	$75
228	Dura Superior	Westland Oil Co., Minot, N.D.	Wht/Grn/Red	SS	50's	$60
229	Dura Superior Extra Long Mileage (script)	Westland Oil Co., Minot, N.D.	Wht/Grn/Red	SS	50's	$60
230	Dura Superior Extra Long Mileage (block)	Westland Oil Co., Minot, N.D.	Wht/Grn/Red	SS	50's	$60
231	Dura Heavy Duty	Westland Oil Co., Minot, N.D.	Wht/Grn/Red	SS	60's	$30
232	Dura Non Detergent	Westland Oil Co., Minot, N.D.	Wht/Grn/Red	SS	60's	$30
233	Dura Motor Oil	Westland Oil Co., Minot, N.D. 58701/Blanchard, La. 71009	Wht/Blu/Red	SS	80's	$30
234	Dura Motor Oil Performance Lubrication	Farstad Oil Co., Minot, N.D.	Wht/Blu/Red	CP	80's	$10
235	EKO-LUB	The Shamrock Oil and Gas Corp., Amarillo, Tx.	Grn/Wht	SS	40's	$75
236	Empire	Wolf's Head Oil Refining Co., Oil City, Pa./N.Y, N.Y.	Blu/Grn/Crm	SS	30's	$100
237	Empire	Wolf's Head Oil Refining Co., Oil City, Pa./N.Y, N.Y.	Chr/Ora/Blu	SS	50's	$35
238	Esso TRI-RAD Anti-freeze	Stanco Inc., Bayway, N.J.	Wht/Red/Blu	SS	1939	$65
239	Esso Anti-freeze Alcohol Type	Esso Standard Oil Co., Linden, N.J.	Wht/Red/Blu	SS	1945	$40
240	Esso ATF (white and red)	no company or location	Wht/Red/Blu	SS	1953	$30
241	Esso ATF (copper and white) SX5c	Humble Oil & Refining Co., Houston, Tx.	Cop/Wht/Red/Blu	SS	1965	$12
242	Esso Aviation (with small wings)	Standard Oil of Pennsylvania, New Jersey, Louisiana (on lid)	Wht/Red/Blu	SS	1938	$300
243	Esso Aviation (with large wings)	Esso Standard Oil Co. (on lid)	Red/Wht/Blu	SS	1945	$250
244	Esso Aviation (with "Made in USA")	Esso Standard Oil Co. (on lid)	Wht/Red/Blu	SS	1957	$40
245	Esso Aviation (without "Made in USA")	Esso Standard Oil Co. (on lid)	Wht/Red/Blu	SS	1959	$40
246	Esso Aviation (silver)	no company or location	Sil/Red/Blu	SS	1952	$40
247	Esso Aviation (grey)	no company or location	Gry/Red/Blu	AL	1953	$40
248	Esso Aviation	Humble Oil & Refining Co., Houston, Tx.	Wht/Red/Blu	SS	1961	$30
249	Esso Aviation (thicker oval, 1 US Quart) S15f	Humble Oil & Refining Co., Houston, Tx	Wht/Red/Blu	SS	1967	$20
250	Esso Aviation E (w/o 1 US Quart,drk blue)S16	Humble Oil & Refining Co.	Wht/Blu/Red	SS	1961	$20
251	Esso Aviation E (w/o 1 US Quart,lt blue)S16b	Humble Oil & Refining Co. Houston, Tx.	Wht/Blu/Red	SS	1963	$20
252	Esso Aviation E (with 1 US Quart) S16e	Humble Oil & Refining Co., Houston, Tx. 77001	Wht/Blu/Red	SS	1967	$20

ALL PRICES LISTED IN THIS BOOK ARE FOR GRADE 9 CANS

225   Diamond Outboard and 2 Cycle: See also 18 All Purpose, 662 Neptune
226-234 Dura: See also 448 Itasca Snomobile
235   Eko-Lub: See also 879-889 Shamrock
236,237 Empire: See also 1156-1165 Wolf's Head
238-252 Esso: See also 10,11 Actol, 171 Challenge, 667 Oilex to 670 Oklahoma Heavy Duty, 672 Palubco, 684 Pate Valve Glide, 1072-1076 Uniflo
241   Esso ATF: This can was made for export.

 225
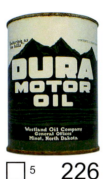 226
 227
 228
 229
 230
 231

 232
 233
 234
 235
 236
 237
 238

 239
 240
 241
 242
 243
 244
 245

 246
 247
 248
 249
 250
 251
 252

#	NAME	COMPANY	COLORS	MAT.	ERA	VALUE
253	Esso Turbo Oil 15	Humble Oil and Refining Co., Houston, Tx.	Ora/Chr/Wht	SS	60's-70's	$15
254	Esso Turbo Oil TJ-15	Humble Oil and Refining Co., Houston, Tx.	Blu/Chr/Wht	SS	60's-70's	$15
255	Esso Turbo Oil 5251	Humble Oil and Refining Co., Houston, Tx.	Gry/Red/Blu/Wht	SS	60's-70's	$15
256	Esso (w/ iceberg and sun) (no US Patent #)	Standard Oil Co. of N.J./Pa./La.	Wht/Red/Blu	SS	8-35	$60
257	Esso (w/ iceberg and sun) (with US Patent)	Standard Oil Co. of N.J./Pa./La.	Wht/Red/Blu	SS	1937	$60
258	Esso Unexcelled (w/ iceberg and sun)	Standard Oil Co. of N.J./Pa./La.	Wht/Red/Blu	SS	12-39	$35
259	Esso Motor Oil	Humble Oil and Refining Co. (on lid)	Wht/Red/Blu	SS	7-47	$20
260	Esso Motor Oil	no company listing	Alu/Red/Blu	AL	50's	$15
261	Esso Motor Oil (S3b) (white w/wide red band)	Humble Oil and Refining Co., Houston, Tx.	Wht/Red/Blu	SS	1963	$12
262	Esso Motor Oil (S3k) (blue with red "Esso")	Humble Oil and Refining Co., Houston, Tx.	Blu/Wht/Red	SS	1965	$8
263	Esso Motor Oil(SX3p) (blue w/white "Esso")	Humble Oil and Refining Co., Houston, Tx. 77001	Blu/Wht	SS	1967	$8
264	Esso Motor Oil (S3p)	Humble Oil and Refining Co., Houston, Tx. 77001	Blu/Wht	CP	1967	$6
265	Essolube (with blue dot)	Colonial Beacon Oil Co., Inc.	Wht/Red/Blu	SS	1-34	$150
266	Essolube (with red dot)	Std. Oil Co. of Pa./N.J./La. (on lid)	Red/Wht	SS	10-36	$25
267	Essolube (with Esso logo)	Esso Standard Oil Co. (on lid)	Red/Wht	SS	40's	$35
268	Esso Essolube	Humble Oil and Refining Co., Houston, Tx.	Wht/Red/Blu	SS	60's	$15
269	Esso Essolube	Humble Oil and Refining Co., Houston, Tx.	Red/Wht	SS	60's	$10
270	Esso Essolube (Sllg) (w/blue oval)	Humble Oil and Refining Co., Houston, Tx.	Red/Wht/Blu	SS	60's	$10
271	Esso Essolube (S11m)	Humble Oil and Refining Co., Houston, Tx. 77001	Red/Wht/Chr	CP	60's	$6
272	Essolube H D	Esso Standard Oil Co.	Red/Wht	SS	6-45	$60
273	Esso Essolube HDX	Humble Oil and Refining Co.	Wht/Red/Blu	AL	60's	$15
274	Esso Essolube HDX (S4)	Humble Oil and Refining Co.	Wht/Red/Blu	SS	60's	$8
275	Esso Essolube HDX (SX4c)	Humble Oil and Refining Co., Houston, Tx.	Grn/Wht/Red/Blu	SS	1964	$8
276	Esso Essolube HDX (S4m)	Humble Oil and Refining Co., Houston, Tx. 77001	Grn/Chr	SS	70's	$6
277	Esso Essolube HDX (S4k)	Humble Oil and Refining Co., Houston, Tx. 77001	Grn/Wht	SS	60's	$8
278	Esso Extra (red top band)	no company listing	Wht/Red/Blu	SS	6-49	$12
279	Esso Extra (white with small "Extra")	no company listing	Wht/Blu/Red	SS	8-50	$8
280	Esso Extra (grey with small "Extra")	no company listing	Gry/Blu/Red	AL	50's	$12

ALL PRICES LISTED IN THIS BOOK ARE FOR GRADE 9 CANS

253-280 Esso: See also 10, 11 Actol, 171 Challenge, 667 Oilex to 670 Oklahoma Heavy Duty, 672 Palubco, 684 Pate Valve Glide, 1072-1076 Uniflo

256   Esso without US Patent number: This variation lists only grades 1,3, and 5 on the side.

257   Esso with US Patent number: This variation lists grades 1,3,5 and 7 on the side along with an Esso Logo

263,275 Esso Motor Oil, Esso Essolube HDX: These cans were for export as designated by the "X" in the can code.

279   Esso Extra: Two other variations of this can exist. In May 1951 the text "A Heavy Duty Motor Oil" was added in white lettering on the side of the August 1950 version.
            In December 1952 the "Zero" and "No. 7" viscosity grades were removed from the side of the can

280   This is an aluminum version of the 1952 version described above.

 ☐ 253
 ☐ 254
 ☐ 255
 ☐⁵ 256
 ☐⁵ 257
 ☐⁵ 258
 ☐⁵ 259

 ☐ 260
 ☐ 261
 ☐ 262
 ☐ 263
 ☐ 264
 ☐⁵ 265
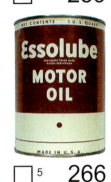 ☐⁵ 266

 ☐⁵ 267
 ☐ 268
 ☐ 269
 ☐ 270
 ☐ 271
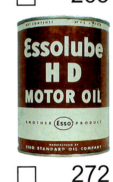 ☐ 272
 ☐ 273

 ☐ 274
 ☐ 275
 ☐ 276
 ☐ 277
 ☐⁵ 278
 ☐⁴,⁵ 279
 ☐⁵ 280

(35)

#	NAME	COMPANY	COLORS	MAT.	ERA	VALUE
281	Esso Extra (with large "Extra")	Humble Oil and Refining Co.	Gry/Blu/Red	AL	1960	$15
282	Esso Extra (with large "Extra")	Humble Oil and Refining Co.	Wht/Blu/Red	SS	1960	$12
283	Esso Extra Multi-Grade (S2s)	Humble Oil and Refining Co., Houston, Tx. 77001	Sil/Blu	CP	70's	$8
284	Esso Extra	Humble Oil and Refining Co., Houston, Tx.	Gld/Red/Wht/Blu	SS	1964	$10
285	Esso Marine	Standard Oil of Pennsylvania/New Jersey (on lid)	Wht/Red/Blu	SS	40's	$50
286	Esso Plus (S450)	Exxon Co., USA, Div. of Exxon Corp., Jouston, Tx. 77252-2180	Gld/Red/Wht/Blu	CP	1978	$10
287	Esso Uniflo (metallic gold)	Esso Standard Oil Co	Wht/Gld/Red/Blu	SS	1952	$15
288	Esso Uniflo (flat gold)	Esso Standard Oil Co.	Wht/Gld/Red/Blu	SS	3-54	$20
289	Esso Uniflo (S1b) (with copper band)	Humble Oil and Refining Co.	Wht/Cop/Blu/Red	SS	60's	$20
290	Esso Uniflo (S1c) (with chrome band)	Humble Oil and Refining Co.	Wht/Chr/Blu/Red	SS	60's	$20
291	Esso Uniflo (S1r)	Humble Oil and Refining Co., Houston, Tx. 77001	Gld/Blu/Wht/Red	SS	60's	$20
292	Esso Uniflo	Humble Oil and Refining Co., Houston, Tx. 77001	Tan/Blu/Wht/Red	PL	1966	$15
293	Everwear	HyVis Oils Inc. of California	Blk/Red/Wht	SS	30's	$55
294	Exceloyl	H.K. Stahl Co., St. Paul, Minn.	Red/Blk/Wht	SS	50's	$45
295	Extralube	National Oil Co., Frenchtown, N.J. 08825	Grn/Red/Wht	SS	60's	$25
296	Extra Lube	Lowe Oil Co., Clinton, Mo.	Red/Yel	SS	60's	$12
297	Extra Lube (Extra Lube in diamond)	Lowe Oil Co., Clinton, Mo.	Red/Yel	SS	60's	$12
298	Facto Multi-Service	B.P Oil Inc., Cleveland, Oh. 44115	Blu/Blk/Wht	SS	80's	$12
299	Facto Supreme	B.P. Oil Inc., Cleveland, Oh. 44115	Blu/Red/Wht	CP	80's	$7
300	Falcon	Oscar Bryant, Hollis, Ok.	Grn/Wht/Red	SS	40's	$10
301	Fina HD Premium	American Petrofina Inc.	Red/Wht/Blu	SS	60's	$25
302	Fina Shield	American Petrofina Inc.	Blu/Wht/Red	SS	60's	$40
303	Fina 10W-30 Special	American Petrofina Inc.	Gld/Red/Blu/Wht	SS	60's	$50
304	Fina Shield ("Non-Detergent" in red)	American Petrofina Inc.	Blu/Wht/Red	CP	60's	$15
305	Fina Permanent Anti-freeze and Coolant	American Petrofina Inc., N.Y.N.Y. 10020	Blu/Wht/Red/Chr	SS	70's	$40
306	Fina Automatic Transmission Fluid	American Petrofina Inc., New York, N.Y. 75221	Grn/Wht/Blu/Red	CP	70's	$7
307	Fina HD Premium	America Petrofina Inc., New York, N.Y. 75221	Red/Wht/Blu/Chr	CP	70's	$5
308	Fina 10W-30 Special	American Petrofina Inc., New York, N.Y.	Gld/Wht/Blu/Red	CP	60's	$10

ALL PRICES LISTED IN THIS BOOK ARE FOR GRADE 9 CANS

281-292 Esso: See also 10,11 Actol, 171 Challenge, 667 Oilex to 670 Oklahoma Heavy Duty, 672 Palubco, 684 Pate Valve Glide, 1072-1076 Uniflo
293 Everwear: See also 416-420 Hyvis
294 Exceloyl: See also 12 Admiral Penn, 99 Arctic Blue Snowmobile Oil, 878 Servoil #2, 1065-1069 Trophy
296,297 Extra Lube: There is a composite version without "reclaimed" and including a zip code. Value $5. See also 174-180 Champion
298,299 Facto, Facto Supreme: See also 117 Boron, 170 Cetron HD, 181 CHD, 365 Golden Duron, 659 Multron, 663, 664 Nitrex, 665 Nitron, 666 Octron, 829-833 Premex, 862, 863 QVO, 895 Sixty Two, 897-917 Sohio
300 Falcon: See also 980 Swift

 281
 282
 ⁴ 283
 ⁴ 284
 285
 286
 ⁵ 287

 ⁵ 288
 ⁴ 289
 ⁴ 290
 ⁴ 291
 292
 293
 294

 295
 296
 297
 298 299

 300
 301

 302
 303
 304
 305
 306
 307
308

㊲

#	NAME	COMPANY	COLORS	MAT.	ERA	VALUE
309	Fina C-T Universal	Fina Oil and Chemical Co., Dallas, Tx. 75206	Yel/Wht/Blu/Red	CP	80's	$4
310	Fina HD Premium	American Petrofina Inc., Dallas, Tx.	Red/Wht/Blu	CP	80's	$5
311	Fina SA Non-Detergent	Fina Oil and Chemical Co., Dallas Tx. 75206	Blu/Wht/Red/Chr	CP	80's	$5
312	Fina Shield ("Non Detergent" in blue)	American Petrofina Inc., Dallas, Tx. 75201	Blu/Wht/Red	CP	70's	$7
313	Fina Ultra Supreme	American Petrofina Inc., Dallas, Tx. 75201	Pur/Wht/Gld/Red	CP	70's	$7
314	Fina Ultra Supreme 10W-40	American Petrofina Inc., Dallas, Tx. 75221	Blu/Wht/Gld/Red	CP	80's	$5
315	Fina 2001 Semi-Synthetic	American Petrofina Inc., Dallas, Tx. 75206	Blu/Red/Wht	CP	70's	$7
316	5 Star	Industrial Lubricants Co., San Antonio, Tx. 78210	Wht/Blu/Sil	CP	80's	$10
317	Fleetwood Aero Craft	Traymore Lubricants, New York	Blu/Wht/Red	SS	40's	$750
318	Ford Anti-freeze M-1186-B	Ford Motor Co., Dearborn, Mich.	Yel/Blu/Red/Wht	SS	30's	$225
319	Fomoco Ethylene Glycol Perm. Anti-freeze	Ford Motor Co., Dearborn, Mich.	Wht/Red	SS	50's	$50
320	Fomoco Methanol Anti-freeze	Ford Motor Co., Dearborn, Mich.	Wht/Red	SS	50's	$50
321	Fomoco Ethylene Glycol Anti-freeze	No company or location listed	Gry/Blu/Wht	SS	60's	$40
322	Ford Anti-freeze and Coolant	Ford Motor Co., Dearborn, Mich. 48121	Blu/Wht/Blu	SS	70's	$15
323	Ford Cooling System Fluid	Ford Marketing Corporation, Dearborn, Mi. 48121	Blu/Wht	SS	5-72	$30
324	Ford Automatic Transmission Fluid	Ford Marketing Corporation, Dearborn, Mi. 48121	Blu/Wht	SS	2-71	$30
325	Ford Premium	Ford Marketing Corporation, Dearborn, Mi. 48121	Wht/Sil/Blk/Blu	SS	7-72	$35
326	Ford Premium SAE 20W-40	Ford Motor Co., Dearborn, Mich. 48121	Wht/Gld/Blk/Blu	CP	7-75	$10
327	Ford Super Premium 6000 mile	Autolite Ford Parts Division, Ford Motor Co., Dearborn, Mi.	Gld/Blu/Wht	SS	1966	$40
328	Ford Super Premium	Ford Marketing Corporation, Dearborn, Mi. 48121	Gld/Wht/Blk/Blu	CP	1966	$15
329	Ford Super Premium SAE 10W-40	Ford Motor Co., Dearborn, Mich. 48121	Gld/Wht/Blk/Blu	CP	7-75	$10
330	Ford 6000 Mile Super Premium	Ford Motor Co., Dearborn, Mi.	Gld/Wht/Blk/Blu	CP	70's	$10
331	Ford Tractor 300	Ford Motor Co., Dearborn, Mi. 48126	Gld/Wht/Blk/Blu	SS	8-70	$15
332	Ford Motorcraft Dexron II ATF	Ford Motor Co., Dearborn, Mi. 48121	Blk/Wht/Ora	CP	80's	$7
333	Ford Motorcraft Premium 20W-40	Ford Motor Co., Dearborn, Mi. 48121	Red/Chr/Blk/Wht	CP	80's	$7
334	Ford Motorcraft Super Duty 15W-40	Ford Motor Co., Dearborn, Mi. 48121	Grn/Chr/Blk/Wht	CP	80's	$7
335	Ford Motorcraft Super Premium 10W-40	Ford Motor Co., Dearborn, Mi. 48121	Gld/Blk/Red/Chr	CP	4-81	$7
336	Ford Motorcraft Super Premium 10W-40	Ford Motor Co., Dearborn, Mi. 48121	Gld/Blk/Red/Chr	CP	4-81	$7

ALL PRICES LISTED IN THIS BOOK ARE FOR GRADE 9 CANS

316   5 Star: See also 95, 96 Approved ATF, 370, 371 Golden State
317   Fleetwood Aero Craft: See also 516 Kenwood
318-336 Ford Anti-freeze to Ford Motorcraft: See also 873, 874 Rotunda
335,336 Ford Motorcraft Super Premium 10W-40: 335 has a silver outline around "Super Premium 10W-40". 336 does not.

☐ 309   ☐ 310   ☐ 311   ☐ 312   ☐ 313   ☐ 314   ☐ 315

☐ 316   ☐ 317   ☐ 318   ☐ 319   ☐ 320   ☐ 321   ☐ 322

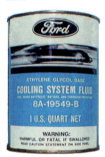   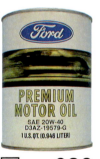   

☐ 323   ☐ 324   ☐ 325   ☐ 326   ☐ 327   ☐ 328   ☐ 329

 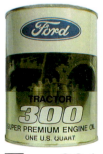     

☐ 330   ☐ 331   ☐ 332   ☐ 333   ☐ 334   ☐ 335   ☐ 336

#	NAME	COMPANY	COLORS	MAT.	ERA	VALUE
337	Fort Pitt	Freedom Oil Co., Freedom, Pa.	Blu/Yel	SS	1936	$350
338	Fox Head Premium	Tritex Petroleum Co., Brooklyn 11, N.Y.	Wht/Red/Blu	SS	60's	$100
339	Freedom F.C.	Freedom Oil Co., Freedom, Pa.	Yel/Blu/Wht	SS	1937	$150
340	Freedom Perfect (with 35 cent price)	Freedom Oil Co., Freedom, Pa.	Yel/Blu/Wht	SS	30's	$325
341	Freedom Perfect ("since 1866")	Freedom-Valvoline Oil Co., Freedom, Pa.	Yel/Blu/Wht	SS	40's	$175
342	Frontier Heavy Duty	Frontier Refining Co.	Wht/Red/Blk	SS	40's	$200
343	Frontier Lube	Frontier Refining Co.	Red/Wht/Blk	SS	50's	$100
344	Frontier Ultra Lube	Frontier Refining Co.	Red/Wht/Blk	SS	50's	$100
345	Frontier Econo Lube	Frontier Refining Co., Denver, Co.	Grn/Wht/Blk/Red	IRS2	50's/60's	$50
346	Frontier Strato Lube Premium	Frontier Refining Co., Denver, Co.	Gld/Wht/Blk/Red	SS	50's/60's	$50
347	Frontier S-3	Frontier Refining Co., Denver ,Co.	Blu/Wht/Blk/Red	IRS2	50's/60's	$150
348	Frontier Ultra Lube	Frontier Refining Co., Denver, Co.	Red/Wht/Blk	SS	50's/60's	$50
349	Frontier Ultra Lube (reverse of 109)	Frontier Refining Co., Denver, Co.	Red/Wht/Gld/Blk	CP	60's	$50
350	Galena	Galena Oil Corporation of Franklin, Pa.	Yel/Blk/Red	SS	30's	$65
351	Super Galena ("Galena Oil Corp.")	Galena Oil Corporation, Franklin, Pa.	Red/Blk/Yel	SS	30's	$45
352	Super Galena ("Galena Division")	Freedom-Valvoline Co., Cincinnati, Oh./Freedom, Pa.	Red/Blk/Yel	SS	40's	$45
353	Gard's Non Detergent High Film Strength	Gard Products Co., Kansas City, Ks.	Grn/Wht/Blu/Chr	CP	60's	$20
354	Gard's All Weather Supreme	Gard Corp., Kansas City, Ks., 66103	Yel/Wht/Ora/Blu	CP	70's	$8
355	Gard's Extra Heavy Duty	Gard Oil Products Inc., Kansas City, Ks. 66110	Ora/Wht/Blu	CP	70's	$8
356	Gard's Non Detergent	Gard Oil Products Inc., Kansas City, Ks. 66110	Grn/Wht/Ora/Blu	CP	70's	$8
357	Gold Bond Triple Refined	no company listed	Wht/Red/Grn	SS	50's	$25
358	Gold Bond Warren's	Warren Oil Co. of Ohio	Grn/Gld/Ora	SS	30's	$40
359	Gold Bond Heavy Duty	Warren Oil Co. (no address listed)	Grn/Gld/Red	SS	50's	$30
360	Gold Bond Extra Heavy Duty	Warren Oil Co., Omaha Neb.	Gld/Red/Wht	SS	60's	$20
361	Gold Bond Dexron II ATF	Warren Oil Co., Omaha, Ne. 68102	Wht/Blk/Gld	CP	70's	$4
362	Gold Bond Type F ATF	Warren Oil Co., Omaha, Ne. 68102	Wht/Blk/Gld	CP	70's	$4
363	Gold-Flo	Peters Oil Co., Milwaukee	Red/Wht/Grn	SS	30's	$60
364	Gold Standard 2000 mile	Bodie-Hoover Petroleum Corp., Chicago, Il.	Gld/Blu/Red	SS	30's	$60

ALL PRICES LISTED IN THIS BOOK ARE FOR GRADE 9 CANS

337 Fort Pitt: See also 107 Beaver Penn, 339-341 Freedom, 350-352 Galena, 1054 Tip Top Penn, 1100-1134 Valvoline
339-341 Freedom: See also 107 Beaver Penn, 337 Fort Pitt, 350-352 Galena, 1054 Tip Top Penn, 1100-1134 Valvoline
342-349 Frontier: See also 108,109 Beeline
350-352 Galena to Super Galena: See also 107 Beaver Penn, 337 Fort Pitt, 339-341 Freedom, 1054 Tip Top Penn, 1100-1134 Valvoline
358,359 Gold Bond Warren's to Gold Bond Heavy Duty: See also 978, 979 Super Power
360-362 Gold Bond Extra Heavy Duty to Gold Bond Type F ATF: See also 102 ATF Automatic Transmission Fluid, 531 Life, 823 Polar Anti-freeze
363 Gold-Flo: See also 757 Peter Penn
364 Gold Standard: See also 657, 658 Motor Seal, 701-704 Pennstate, and 705, 706 Pennsyline

 337
 338
 339
 340
 341
 342
 343

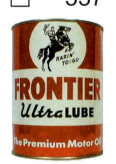 344
 345
 346
 347
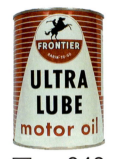 348
 349
 350

 351
 352
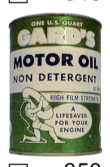 353
 354
 355
 356
 357

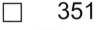
 358

 359 360 361 362
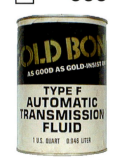 363
 364

#	NAME	COMPANY	COLORS	MAT.	ERA	VALUE
365	Golden Duron	Boron Oil Co., Cleveland, Oh.44115 (on bottom lid)	Gld/Wht/Pur	SS	70's	$25
366	Golden Eagle	Century-Morrison Oil Co., Dallas, Tx	Grn/Yel	SS	40's	$250
367	Golden Eagle	Idaho Refining Co./ Wasatch Refining Co./Inland Empire Refining Co.	Red/Yel/Blu	SS	40's	$500
368	Golden State Quality Lubrications	no company listed	Pur/Ora	CP	60's	$6
369	Golden State ATF	Golden State Products, Clinton, Mo.	Gld/Blk/Wht/Yel	CP	70's	$5
370	Golden State (with Texas map)	Industrial Lubricants Co., San Antonio, Tx. 78220	Sil/Blu	CP	70's	$12
371	Golden State	Industrial Lubricants Co., San Antonio, Tx. 78210	Gld/Blk/Wht/Sil	CP	80's	$5
372	Griffin's Guranteed High Quality	Griffin Grocery Co., Ok/Ark/Tx	Wht/Blu/Red	SS	40's	$35
373	Griffin's Guranteed Highest Quality	Griffin Grocery Co., Ok/Ark/Tx	Red/Wht/Blu	SS	40'S	$25
374	Harbor Non-Detergent	Harbor Stations, Tulsa, Ok.	Grn/Chr/Blk/Red	RS	60's	$125
375	Harley-Davidson(w/oval "O" and 85 grade)	Harley Davidson Motor Co., Milwaukee Wis.	Blk/Yel/Wht	SS	30's	$200
376	Harley-Davidson (w/ round "O" and 75 grade)	Harley Davidson Motor Co., Milwaukee Wis.	Blk/Ora/Wht	SS	40's	$150
377	Harley-Davidson 4-Cycle Motors	Harley Davidson Motor Co., Milwaukee Wis.	Wht/Ora/Blk	SS	50's	$175
378	Harley-Davidson Gunk Motorcycle Cleaner	Harley Davidson Motor Co., Milwaukee, Wis.	Wht/Ora/Blk	SS	50's	$150
379	Harley-Davidson Pre-Luxe	Harley Davidson Motor Co., Milwaukee, Wis.	Wht/Blk/Yel	SS	50's	$75
380	Harley-Davidson Pre-Luxe	Harley Davidson Motor Co., Milwaukee, Wis.	Wht/Ora/Blk	SS	60's	$50
381	Harley-Davidson Racing	Harley Davidson Motor Co. Inc., Milwaukee, Wis. 52301	Wht/Ora/Blk	SS	60's	$60
382	Harley-Davidson Pre-Luxe (w/motorcycle)	Harley Davidson Motor Co. Inc., Milwaukee, Wis. 53201	Ora/Wht/Blk	SS	70's	$40
383	Harley-Davidson Premium Grade	Harley Davidson Motor Co. Inc., Milwaukee, Wis. 52301	Ora/Wht/Blk	CP	70's	$25
384	Harley-Davidson Sno-Oil	Harley Davidson Motor Co. Inc., Milwaukee, Wis. 52301	Ora/Wht/Blk	SS	70's	$60
385	Harley-Davidson Two-Cycle SAE 40	Harley Davidson Motor Co. Inc., Milwaukee, Wis. 53201	Ora/Wht/Blk	SS	70's	$40
386	Harley-Davidson Pre-Luxe Grade	AMF/Harley Davidson Motor Co. Inc., Milwaukee, Wis. 53201	Ora/Wht/Blu	CP	70's	$12
387	Harley-Davidson Power Blend	Harley Davidson Motor Co., Milwaukee, Wis. 53201	Gry/Blk/Wht	CP	70's	$12
388	Harley-Davidson Premium II	Harley-Davidson Motor Co. Parts & Accesories Div., Milwaukee, Wis. 53201	Ora/Blk/Wht	CP	80's	$10
389	Harvest King All Season	Mid-States Distributing Co. Inc., St. Paul Mn. 55116	Wht/Gld/Grn	CP	80's	$5
390	Harvest King Heavy Duty	Mid-States Distributing Co. Inc., St. Paul Mn. 55116	Wht/Gld/Blu	CP	80's	$5
391	Harvest King Non Detergent	Mid-States Distributing Co. Inc., St. Paul Mn. 55116	Wht/Gld/Red	CP	80's	$5
392	Harvest King Automatic Transmission Fluid	Mid-States Distributing Co. Inc., St. Paul Mn. 55116	Wht/Gld/Blk	CP	80's	$5

ALL PRICES LISTED IN THIS BOOK ARE FOR GRADE 9 CANS

365   Golden Duron: See also 117 Boron, 170 Cetron HD, 181 CHD, 298, 299 Facto, 659 Multron, 663, 664 Nitrex, 665 Nitron, 666 Octron, 829-833 Premex, 862, 863 QVO, 895 Sixty Six, 897-917 Sohio

367   Golden Eagle: See also 434 Indian Penn

370, 371 Golden State: See also 95, 96 Approved ATF, 316 5 Star

375, 376 Harley-Davidson: The difference between 375 and 376 is 375 uses an oval shaped "0" In "Harley Davidson Motorcycle Oil" and the Medium Heavy grade of oil is listed as 85. 376 uses a round "O", and the Medium Heavy Grade is listed as 75.

 365
 366
 367
 368
 369
 370
 371

 372
 373
 374
 375
 376
 377
 378

 379
 380
 381
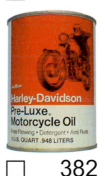 382
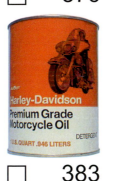 383
 384
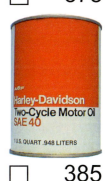 385

 386
 387
 388
 389
 390
 391
 392

#	NAME	COMPANY	COLORS	MAT.	ERA	VALUE
393	Harvest Supreme Non Detergent	T.S.C. Ind., St. Cloud, Minn. 56301	Blu/Wht/Red/Chr	CP	70's	$15
394	HD Heavy Duty H.D.D.	Wright Oil Co., San Antonio, Tx.	Wht/Blu/Red	SS	60's	$40
395	HD Value Plus	Hinky Dinky	Wht/Red/Blu	SS	60's	$30
396	Hercules Premium Quality	Dryer,Clark & Dryer Oil Co., Oklahoma City	Wht/Red/Blu	SS	50's	$50
397	Hercules	Dryer,Clark & Dryer Oil Co., Oklahoma City	Wht/Red/Blu	SS	50's	$25
398	High Penn	High Penn Oil Co., High Point, N.C.	Wht/Grn/Red	SS	60's	$20
399	Homelite Chain Saw Oil	Homelite, Port Chester, N.Y.	Red/Grn/Wht	SS	60's	$10
400	Homelite 2 Cycle SAE 30	Homelite, A Textron Div., Port Chester, N.Y. 10573	Blu/Red/Wht	SS	70's	$10
401	Homoco Treat-O-Film	Home Oil Co., Wichita, Ks.	Red/Blu/Wht	SS	50's	$40
402	Homoco Treat-O-Film	Home Oil Co., Wichita, Ks.	Red/Blu/Chr	SS	50's	$35
403	Hoosier Pete 100	Hoosier Petroleum Co. Inc., Indianapolis, Ind.	Grn/Sil/Blk/Red	SS	50's	$100
404	HPX Horse Power Multiplied	J.D. Street and Co. Inc., St. Louis, Mo.	Wht/Ora/Blu	SS	50's	$25
405	Hudson (with tanker, race cars, planes)	Hudson Oil Co., Kansas City	Red/Wht/Blk	SS	50's	$300
406	Hudson Premium (w/tanker,race cars,planes)	Hudson Oil Co., Kansas City	Gld/Blu/Red	SS	50's	$300
407	Hudson's Finest Pennvein	Hudson Oil Co., General Offices Kansas City	Red/Blk/Wht	SS	40's	$225
408	Hudson (with tanker)	Hudson Oil Co., Kansas City	Red/Wht/Blk	AL	60's	$75
409	Hudson (with tanker)	Hudson Oil Co., Kansas City	Red/Chr/Blk	SS	60's	$75
410	Hudson (with tanker)	Hudson Oil Co., Kansas City	Red/Alu/Blk	AL	60's	$75
411	Hudson Premium (with tanker)	Hudson Oil Co., Kansas City	Gld/Alu/Blk	AL	60's	$75
412	Hudson ATF	Hudson Oil Co. of Delaware Inc., Kansas City	Sil/Yel/Blk	CP	70's	$12
413	Hudson ATF Dexron	Hudson Oil Co., Kansas City, Ks. 66103	Yel/Chr/Blk	CP	80's	$8
414	Hudson High Detergent	Hudson Oil Co., Kansas City, Ks. 66103	Red/Chr/Blk	CP	80's	$8
415	Hydra-Flo ATF Type A	Pennzoil Division, South Penn Oil Co., Oil City, Pa.	Red/Yel/Blk	SS	50's	$20
416	Hy Vis Mileage Metered	HyVis Oils Inc., Warren, Pa.	Blk/Wht/Yel/Red	SS	30's	$45
417	Hy Vis Super Refined 100% Pure Penn.	HyVis Oils, New York, N.Y.	Blk/Wht/Red/Yel	SS	40's	$35
418	Hy Vis Premium	HyVis Oils Inc., New York, N.Y.	Blk/Wht/Red/Yel	SS	40's	$35
419	HyVis Oils	HyVis Oils, New York, N.Y.	Blk/Wht/Red	SS	60's	$20
420	HyVis Oils	HyVis Oils, New York, N.Y.	Blk/Chr/Red	CP	60's	$10

ALL PRICES LISTED IN THIS BOOK ARE FOR GRADE 9 CANS

396,397 Hercules: See also 650-653 Mother Penn
398   High Penn: See also 870 Rex, 1057 Triple A
404   HPX: See also 694 Penndurol, 1168-1174 Zephyr
405-414 Hudson-Hudson High Detergent: See also 533-535 LLL
415   Hydra-Flo: See also 682 Par-O-Vis, 683 Super Par-O-Vis, 708-750 Pennzoil, 1055, 1056 Tranzport, 1175 Zoildeez, 1176 Zoilube
416-420 Hy Vis Mileage Metered to Hy Vis Oils: See also 293 Everwear

 393
 394
 395
 396
 397
 398
 399
 400
 401
 402
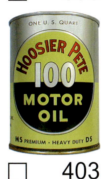 403
 404
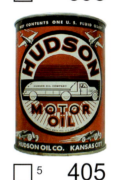 405
 406
 407
 408
 409
 410
 411
 412
 413
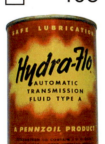 414
 415
 416
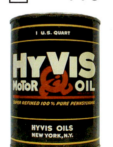 417
 418
 419
 420

#	NAME	COMPANY	COLORS	MAT.	ERA	VALUE
421	I.H. Hy-Tran Fluid	International Harvester Co., Chicago Il., 60611	Red/Wht/Blk	CP	70's	$5
422	I.H. Inter Season	International Harvester Co., Chicago, Il. 60611	Wht/Pur/Blk/Red	CP	70's	$5
423	I.H. Low Ash	International Harvester Co., Chicago, Il. 60611	Blu/Wht/Blk/Red	CP	70's	$5
424	I.H. No.1 For Diesel Engines	I.H. Co., Chicago, Ill. 60611	Gld/Wht/Blk/Red	CP	70's	$5
425	I.H. No.1 For Diesel Engines 15W-40	I.H. Co., 401 N. Michigan Ave., Chicago, Il. 60611	Gld/Sil/Blk/Red	CP	80's	$4
426	I.H. No. 1	International Harvester Co., Chicago, Il. 60611	Red/Wht/Blk	CP	70's	$5
427	Imperial Premium	Johnson Oil Co. State Distributors, Mt. Pleasant, Mich.	Tan/Red/Blk	SS	50's	$60
428	Index Re-Refined from Used Oil	Gopher State Oil Co., Minneapolis, Mn.	Red/Wht	SS	60's	$25
429	Index Re-Refined	no company or location listed	Red/Wht	SS	60's	$20
430	Indian (with full color head)	Indian Motorcycle Co., Springfield, Mass.	Yel/Red/Blk/Wht	SS	30's	$300
431	Indian (with red head)	Indian Motorcycle Co., Springfield, Mass.	Yel/Red	SS	40's	$250
432	Indian Premium	The Indian Co., Springfield, Mass.	Yel/Red/Wht	SS	40's	$250
433	Indian Premium (with "NEW")	The Indian Co., Springfield, Mass	Red/Wht/Blk	SS	50's	$200
434	Indian Penn	Idaho Refining Co., Wasatch Refining Co., Inland Empire Refining Co.	Yel/Red/Blu	SS	40's	$1250
435	Inter-State XL Motor Oil (with orange lines)	Inter-state Oil Co., Kansas City	Wht/Yel/Ora/Blu	SS	30's	$125
436	Inter-State XL Motor Oil	Inter-State Oil Co., Kansas City	Wht/Yel/Blu/Ora	SS	40's	$85
437	Inter-State XL-Penn Motor Oil	Inter-State Oil Co., Kansas City	Wht/Yel/Blu/Ora	SS	40's	$100
438	Inter-State X-L Oils	Inter-State Oil Co., Kansas City	Wht/Blu/Ora	SS	50's	$65
439	Inter-State XLR8 Premium Non Detergent	Inter-State Oil Co. Inc., Kansas City, Ks.	Red/Blu/Wht	SS	60's	$40
440	Inter-State XLR8 H.D. Multi Grade All Season	Inter-State Oil Co. Inc., 87 Shawnee Ave, Kansas City, Ks. 66119	Wht/Red/Blu	CP	60's	$7
441	Inter-State XLR8 Two Cycle Outboard	Inter-State Oil Co. Inc., 87 Shawnee Ave, Kansas City, Ks. 66119	Wht/Blu/Red	CP	60's	$20
442	Inter-State Oil All Season Heavy Duty	Inter-State Oil Co. Inc., Kansas City, Ks. 66119	Red/Blu/Wht	CP	70's	$7
443	Inter-State Oil Ford ATF	Inter-State Oil Co. Inc., 87 Shawnee Ave, Kansas City, Ks. 66119	Blu/Wht/Red	CP	70's	$8
444	Inter-State Oil Type F ATF (w/large shield)	Inter-State Oil Co. Inc., Kansas City, Ks. 66119	Wht/Blu/Red	CP	80's	$5
445	Inter-State Oil Type F ATF (w/small shield)	Inter-State Oil Co. Inc., Kansas City, Ks. 66119	Wht/Blu/Red	CP	80's	$3
446	Inter-State Oil Dexron II ATF	Inter-State Oil Co. Inc., Kansas City, Ks. 66119	Wht/Red/Blu	CP	80's	$3
447	Inter-State All Season	Inter-State Oil Co. Inc, 301 E. Donovan Rd., Kansas City, Ks. 66115	Wht/Gld/Blu/Red	CP	80's	$5
448	Itasca Snomobile	Itasca Products Div., Westland Oil Co., Minot, N.D./Blanchard, La.	Pur/Wht	SS	60's	$45

ALL PRICES LISTED IN THIS BOOK ARE FOR GRADE 9 CANS

421-426 I.H. Hy-Tran Fluid to IH No.1: See also 130-136 Case/IH
430-433 Indian to Indian Premium (with "NEW"): See also 129 C.A.M.
434   Indian Penn: See also 367 Golden Eagle
435-447 Inter-State XL Motor Oil (wth orange lines) to Interstate All Season: See also 84 AP Type A ATF, 660, 661 National Special
448   Itasca Snomobile: See also 226-234 Dura

 421
 422
 423
 424
 425
 426
 427

 428
 429
 430
 431
 432
 433
 434

 435
 436
 437
 438
 439
 440
 441

 442
 443
 444
 445
 446
447
448

#	NAME	COMPANY	COLORS	MAT.	ERA	VALUE
449	Jay-Dee	The Delong Co., Clinton, Wis/Chicago Il.	Wht/Red/Blu	SS	40's	$65
450	Jayhawk Oils	Kent Oil Co., Salina, Ks.	Wht/Blu/Red/Yel	SS	40's	$850
451	Jayhawk Oils H-D-	Kent Oil Co., Salina, Ks.	Wht/Blu/Red/Yel	SS	40's	$950
452	Jayhawks Petroleum Product	Time Oil Co., Tacoma, Wn.	Yel/Wht/Blk	CP	80's	$20
453	J.C. Penny 10W-30	J.C. Penny Co. Inc., New York, N.Y. 10019	Chr/Blk	CP	80's	$8
454	J.C. Penny Premium 10W-40	J.C. Penny Co. Inc., New York, N.Y. 10019	Gld/Blk	CP	80's	$8
455	J.C. Penny Heavy Duty	J.C. Penny Co. Inc., New York, N.Y. 10019	Blu/Wht/Chr	CP	80's	$8
456	J.C. Penny Automatic Transmission Fluid	J.C. Penny Co. Inc., New York, N.Y. 10019	Grn/Wht/Blk	CP	80's	$8
457	K-24	Bradford Oil Refining Co., Bradford, Pa.	Blk/Gld	SS	40's	$60
458	Kan-O-Gold	Universal Motor Oils Co. Wichita, Ks.	Wht/Blk/Gld	SS	50's	$30
459	Kan-O-Gold	Universal Motor Oils Co. Inc., Wichita, Ks.	Gld/Chr/Blk/Wht	RS	60's	$25
460	Kan-O-Gold	Universal Motor Oils Co. Inc., Wichita, Ks.	Gld/Sil/Red/Wht	RS	60's	$25
461	Kan-O-Gold	Universal Motor Oil Co., Wichita, Ks.67219	Gld/Sil/Blk	CP	70's	$6
462	Kawasaki 2 Cycle	Kawasaki Motors Corp. USA, Santa Ana, Ca.	Wht/Yel/Grn/Blk	CP	80's	$8
463	Kendall (w/o 2,000 mile edge bands)	Kendall Refining Co., Bradford, Pa.	Red/Wht/Blk	SS	1933	$50
464	Kendall (no prop, both car tires are visible)	Kendall Refining Co., Bradford, Pa.	Red/Wht/Blk	SS	34-38	$40
465	Kendall (no prop,front car tire only is visible)	Kendall Refining Co., Bradford, Pa.	Red/Wht/Blk	SS	39-42	$35
466	Kendall (with prop on plane)	Kendall Refining Co., Bradford, Pa.	Red/Wht/Blk	SS	46-57	$30
467	Kendall The 2000 mile Oil (w/o cars,planes)	Kendall Refining Co., Bradford, Pa.	Red/Sil/Blk	SS	1958	$20
468	Kendall Dual Action The 2000 mile Oil	Kendall Refining Co., Bradford, Pa.	Red/Wht	SS	59-63	$20
469	Kendall Dual Action (w/o The 2000 mile Oil)	Kendall Refining Co., Bradford, Pa.	Red/Wht	CP	1964	$15
470	Kendall Superb	Kendall Refining Co., Bradford, Pa.	Red/Sil/Wht/Blk	SS	53-58	$20
471	Kendall Superb	Kendall Refining Co., Bradford, Pa.	Red/Gry/Wht	AL	59-60	$25
472	Kendall Superb	Kendall Refining Co., Bradford, Pa.	Wht/Gld/Gry/Red	SS	61-63	$20
473	Kendall Quality Lubricants	Kendall Refining Co., Bradford, Pa.	Red/Wht/Blk	SS	46-50's	$20
474	Kendall Quality Lubricants	Kendall Refining Co., Bradford, Pa.	Red/Sil/Blk	SS	46-50's	$20
475	Kendall Specialized Lubricants	Kendall Refining Co., Bradford, Pa.	Red/Wht	SS	50's-63	$20
476	Kendall Non Detergent (with Penn. map)	Kendall Refining Co., Bradford, Pa.	Blk/Sill/Red	SS	55-59	$20

ALL PRICES LISTED IN THIS BOOK ARE FOR GRADE 9 CANS

457   K-24: See also 16,17 Allpen
458-461 Kan-O-Gold: See also 221-224 Dezol, 876 Ser-Vis, 1083-1099 Universal
466   Kendall has 5 variations. 1946-52: (1) Refined and reinforced for passenger car..., (2) Refined and reinforced with carefully selected, metal seam, (3) Same as 2 except has a white seam and "Motor Oil" in black, (4) Same as 3 except the words "selected" and "gasoline" are hyphenated. 1952-57 version has ".946 liter" added.
467   Kendall The 2000 mile Oil has two variations. One has "Made in USA" on the side while the other doesn't have this.
468   Kendall Dual Action has two variations in the writing on the side of the can. (1) "Gives oustanding performance..." (2) "Exceeds car manufacturer's..."
475   Kendall Specialized Lubricants has 2 composite variations. 1964: (1) Aluminum lid and bottom (experimental version) (2) Steel lid and bottom.
476   Kendall Non Detergent has 2 variations. (1) "For use in aviation,automotive,LPG, and other engines..." (2) "For use in aviation,automotive and other engines..."

 □ 449
 □ 450
 □ 451
 □ 452
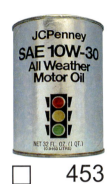 □ 453
 □ 454
 □ 455

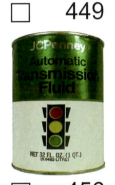 □ 456
 □ 457
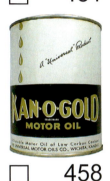 □ 458
 □ 459
 □ 460
 □ 461
 □ 462

 □5 463
 □5 464
 □5 465
 □5 466
 □5 467
 □ 4, 5 468
 □4 469

 □5 470
 □5 471
 □5 472
 □ 473
 □ 474
 □ 475
 □5 476

(49)

#	NAME	COMPANY	COLORS	MAT.	ERA	VALUE
477	Kendall Non-Detergent (without Penn. map)	Kendall Refining Co., Bradford, Pa.	Blk/Sil/Red	SS	60-63	$20
478	Kendall Automatic Transmission Fluid	Kendall Refining Co., Bradford, Pa.	Red/Wht/Blk	SS	50-58	$25
479	Kendall A-T Fluid	Kendall Refining Co., Bradford, Pa.	Red/Wht	SS	59-63	$20
480	Kendall M-6 "The 6 month Motor Oil"	Kendall Refining Co., Bradford, Pa.	Blk/Red/Gld	CP	64-68	$12
481	Kendall M-6	Kendall Refining Co., Div. of Witco Chemical Corp., Bradford, Pa. 16701	Blk/Wht/Gld/Red	CP	73-74	$10
482	Kendall Non-Detergent	Kendall Refining Co., Div. of Witco Chemical Corp., Bradford, Pa. 16701	Blu/Wht/Gld/Red	CP	64-72,76	$10,$6
483	Kendall Non-Detergent 100% Pennsylvania	Kendall Refining Co., Div. of Witco Chemical Corp., Bradford, Pa. 16701	Blu/Wht/Gld/Red	CP	73-74	$7
484	Kendall A-T Fluid	Kendall Refining Co., Div. of Witco Chemical Corp., Bradford, Pa. 16701	Grn/Wht/Gld/Red	CP	64-72,76	$10,$6
485	Kendall Dual Action (w/o "1 U.S. Fluid Quart")	Kendall Refining Co., Bradford, Pa.	Red/Wht/Gld	CP	1964	$12
486	Kendall Dual Action (with "1 U.S. Fluid Quart")	See note below for variations	Red/Wht/Gld	CP	64-72,76	$10,$6
487	Kendall Dual Action 100% Pennsylvania	Kendall Refining Co., Div. of Witco Chemical Corp., Bradford, Pa. 16701	Red/Wht/Gld	CP	73-74	$7
488	Kendall Dual Action Pennsylvania	Kendall Refining Co., Div. of Witco Chemical Corp., Bradford, Pa. 16701	Red/Wht/Gld	CP	1975	$7
489	Kendall Snowmobile 100% Pennsylvania	Kendall Refining Co., Div. of Witco Chemical Corp., Bradford, Pa. 16701	Wht/Red/Blu	CP	73-74	$20
490	Kendall Specialized	Kendall Refining Co., Div. of Witco Chemical Corp., Bradford, Pa. 16701	Brn/Red/Gld/Wht	CP	65-72,76`	$10,$6
491	Kendall Superb	Kendall Refining Co., Div. of Witco Chemical Corp., Bradford, Pa. 16701	Wht/Red/Gld	CP	1964-72	$7
492	Kendall Superb 100% Pennsylvania	Kendall Refining Co., Div. of Witco Chemical Corp., Bradford, Pa. 16701	Wht/Red/Gld	CP	73-74	$7
493	Kendall Superb Multi-Vis Pennsylvania	Kendall Refining Co., Div. of Witco Chemical Corp., Bradford, Pa. 16701	Blk/Wht/Gld/Red	CP	1975	$7
494	Kendall Superb Multi-Vis	Kendall Refining Co., Div. of Witco Chemical Corp., Bradford, Pa. 16701	Blk/Gld/Wht/Red	CP	1976	$8
495	Kendall GT-1 Racing Oil	Kendall Refining Co., Div. of Witco Chemical Corp., Bradford, Pa. 16701	Gld/Blk/Wht/Red	CP	65,66-72	$20,$15
496	Kendall GT 1 Racing Oil 100% Pennsylvania	Kendall Refining Co., Div. of Witco Chemical Corp., Bradford, Pa. 16701	Gld/Blk/Wht/Red	CP	73-74	$12
497	Kendall GT 1 Racing Oil Pennsylvania	Kendall Refining Co., Div. of Witco Chemical Corp., Bradford, Pa. 16701	Gld/Blk/Wht/Red	CP	1975	$12
498	Kendall GT-1 Motor Oil (with red "GT-1")	Kendall Refining Co., Div. of Witco Chemical Corp., Bradford, Pa. 16701	Gld/Blk/Wht/Red	CP	1976	$15
499	Kendall GT-1 Special Motorcycle 100% Penn.	Kendall Refining Co., Div. of Witco Chemical Corp., Bradford, Pa. 16701	Blu/Blk/Wht/Red	CP	73-74	$15
500	Kendall GT-1 Special Motorcycle Penn.	Kendall Refining Co., Div. of Witco Chemical Corp., Bradford, Pa. 16701	Blu/Blk/Wht/Red	CP	1975	$15
501	Kendall Dual Action Heavy Duty	Kendall Refining Co., Div. of Witco Chemical Corp., Bradford, Pa. 16701	Red/Wht/Gld	CP	77-85	$4
502	Kendall GT-1 High Performance	Kendall Refining Co., Div. of Witco Chemical Corp., Bradford, Pa. 16701	Gld/Blk/Red/Wht	CP	77-85	$4
503	Kendall Motorcycle	Kendall Refining Co., Div. of Witco Chemical Corp., Bradford, Pa. 16701	Blu/Blk/Gld/Wht	CP	77-85	$8
504	Kendall Non Detergent	Kendall Refining Co., Div. of Witco Chemical Corp., Bradford, Pa. 16701	Blu/Gld/Wht	CP	77-85	$4

ALL PRICES LISTED IN THIS BOOK ARE FOR GRADE 9 CANS

477   Kendall Non-Detergent has a composite version issued in 1964. $12
482,484 Kendall Non-Detergent, Kendall A-T Fluid have two variations. 1964-72 has the PGCOA #3 information on the side. 1976 version does not.
486   Kendall Dual Action has three variations. 1964-65 Kendall Ref. Co., 1966-72 Kendall Ref. Co., Div. of Witco, 1976 version lacks the PGCOA #3 identification.
490   Kendall Specialized has two variations. 1965-72 has the PGCOA #3 information on the side. 1976 version does not.
495   Kendall GT-1 Racing Oil has two variations. 1965 Kendall Refining Co., 1966-72 Kendall Refining Co., Div. of Witco
501-504 These cans have three variations in the wording on the side. 1977-78, 79-81 and 82-85
Note: Variations for 477-485 cans are as folows: 477-478 has Exceeds all car manufacturers warranty requirements, maintain proper oil level., 479-481 has in addition Don't Pollute-Conserve..., Return used oil..., Protect our environment, Dispose of used oil properly. 482-485 deletes the Exceeds all car manufacturers warrenty requirements.

 □⁴ 477
 □⁵ 478
 □ 479
 □ 480
 □ 481
 □ 482
 □ 483

 □⁴ 484
 □⁴ 485
 □ 486
 □⁴ 487
 □⁴ 488
 □ 489
 □ 490

 □⁴ 491
 □⁴ 492
 □⁴ 493
 □ 494
 □ 495
 □ 496
 □ 497

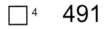
 □ 498
□ 499
□ 500
 □⁴ 501
 □ 502
 □ 503
 □ 504

#	NAME	COMPANY	COLORS	MAT.	ERA	VALUE
505	Kendall Automatic Transmission Fluid	Kendall Refining Co., Div. of Witco Chemical Corp., Bradford, Pa. 16701	Grn/Gld/Wht/Red	CP	77-83	$7
506	Kendall Specialized	Kendall Refining Co., Div. of Witco Chemical Corp., Bradford, Pa. 16701	Brn/Wht/Gld/Red	CP	77-85	$4
507	Kendall Super DSL	Kendall Refining Co., Div. of Witco Chemical Corp., Bradford, Pa. 16701	Red/Gld/Wht	CP	78-85	$7
508	Kendall Superb 10W-30 All Seasons	Kendall Refining Co., Div. of Witco Chemical Corp., Bradford, Pa. 16701	Blk/Gld/Wht/Red	CP	77-81	$6
509	Kendall Superb 10W-40 All Seasons	Kendall Refining Co., Div. of Witco Chemical Corp., Bradford, Pa. 16701	Blk/Gld/Wht/Red	CP	77-81	$6
510	Kendall Superb 20W-40 All Seasons	Kendall Refining Co., Div. of Witco Chemical Corp., Bradford, Pa. 16701	Blk/Gld/Wht/Red	CP	77-85	$6
511	Kendall Superb 20W-50 All Seasons	Kendall Refining Co., Div. of Witco Chemical Corp., Bradford, Pa. 16701	Blk/Gld/Wht/Red	CP	77-85	$6
512	Kendall Superb 100 5W-30	Kendall Refining Co., Div. of Witco Chemical Corp., Bradford, Pa. 16701	Blk/Wht/Sil/Red	CP	80-85	$5
513	Kendall Superb 100 10W-30	Kendall Refining Co., Div. of Witco Chemical Corp., Bradford, Pa. 16701	Blk/Wht/Sil/Red	CP	80-85	$5
514	Kendall Superb 100 10W-40	Kendall Refining Co., Div. of Witco Chemical Corp., Bradford, Pa. 16701	Blk/Wht/Sil/Red	CP	80-85	$4
515	Kendall 5W-40 Synthetic	Kendall Refining Co., Div. of Witco Chemical Corp., Bradford, Pa. 16701	Sil/Blk/Red/Wht	CP	78-81	$6
516	Kenwood	Traymore Lubricants, New York, N.Y.	Blu/Wht/Red	SS	30's	$40
517	Klotz Chemical Racing Lubricant	Klotz Special Formula Products Inc., Ft Wayne, In. 46801	Red/Wht/Blk	SS	70's	$20
518	Klotz Techniplate 2 Cycle Racing	Klotz Special Formula Products Inc., Ft Wayne, In. 46801	Red/Wht/Blk	SS	70's	$20
519	K Mart ATF (Net 32 oz.... text in red)	S.S. Kresge Co., Troy, Michigan 48084	Wht/Blk/Red/Gld	CP	80's	$4
520	K Mart ATF (Net 32 oz.... text in black)	S.S. Kresge Co., Troy, Michigan 48084	Wht/Blk/Red/Gld	CP	80's	$4
521	K Mart Deluxe 10W-40	S.S. Kresge Co., Troy, Michigan 48084	Wht/Gld/Blk/Red	CP	80's	$4
522	K Mart Heavy Duty Detergent	S.S. Kresge Co., Troy, Michigan 48084	Blu/Wht/Blk/Gld	CP	70's	$4
523	K Mart Non-Detergent	S.S. Kresge Co., Troy, Michigan 48084	Red/Wht/Blk/Gld	CP	70's	$4
524	K Mart Super 10W-30	S.S. Kresge Co., Troy, Michigan 48232	Gld/Wht/Blk/Red	CP	80's	$4
525	K Mart Dexron II ATF	K Mart Corporation, Troy, Mich. 48084	Wht/Blu/Red/Gld	CP	70's	$4
526	K Mart SAE 20W50 4 Cycle	K Mart Corporation, Troy, Mich. 48084	Wht/Blk/Blu/Gld	CP	70's	$4
527	K Mart Super Life 10W40	K Mart Corporation, Troy, Mich. 48084	Yel/Wht/Blk/Red	CP	80's	$4
528	Kunzoil	The Kunz Oil Co., Minneapolis	Yel/Grn/Red	SS	40's	$400
529	Liberty	Liberty Oil Co., Des Moines, Ia.	Wht/Red/Blk	SS	40's	$50
530	Liberty Bond	R.E. Moore Co., Tyler, Tx.	Red/Wht	SS	30's	$35
531	Life Re-Refined (with "NEW")	Warren Oil Co., Omaha, Neb.	Wht/Red/Blu	SS	50's	$40
532	Liquid Gold	Consumers Oil Co. (no location)	Chr/Blu	RS	50's	$100

ALL PRICES LISTED IN THIS BOOK ARE FOR GRADE 9 CANS

505,506,510,511 Kendall ATF, Specialized, Superb 20W-40, Superb 20W-50 have three variations in the wording on the side. 1977-78,79-81 and 82-85
507   Kendall Super DSL has three variations. 1978,79-81, and 82-85
508,509 Kendall Superb 10W-30 All Seasons, 10W-40 All Seasons has two variations of wording on the side. 1977-78 and 1979-81
512-514 Kendall Superb 100 5W-30, Superb 100 10W-30, Superb 100 10W-40 have two variations in the wording on the side. 1980-81 and 82-85
515   Kendall Synthetic 5W-40 has two variations. 1978 and 1979-81
516   Kenwood: See also 317 Fleetwood Aero Craft
530   Liberty Bond: See also 867 Remco, 871 Rich-Tane
531   Life Re-Refined (with "NEW"): See also 102 ATF Automatic Transmission Fluid, 360 Gold Bond Extra Heavy Duty to 362 Gold Bond ATF, 823 Polar Anti-freeze

 505
 506
 507
 508
 509
 510
 511
 512
 513
 514
 515
 516
 517
 518
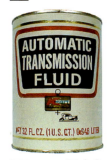 519
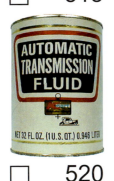 520
 521
 522
 523
 524
 525
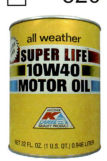 526
 527
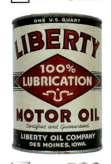 528
 529
 530
 531

 532

#	NAME	COMPANY	COLORS	MAT.	ERA	VALUE
533	LLL Long Life Lube (w/planes, car, truck)	no company or location listed	Red/Blk/Wht	SS	40's	$250
534	LLL Long Life Lube	Hudson Oil Co., Kansas City	Grn/Alu/Blk	AL	60's	$85
535	LLL Long Life Lube	Hudson Oil Co., Kansas City	Grn/Chr/Blk	SS	60's	$85
536	Lovolene	Loving's Oil and Gas Co., 4600 East Grand Ave., Dallas, Tx.	Wht/Red/Blu	SS	40's	$50
537	Lubomatic ATF Type A-Suffix A	Petroleum Chemicals & Specialties Co., L.A. Cal. 90023	Gld/Blk/Red	CP	80's	$4
538	Lubrimatic ATF Type A	Prarie States Oil & Grease Co.,Danville In.	Wht/Blu/Red	SS	60's	$15
539	Lubriplate H.D.S.	Fiske Brothers Refining Co., Newark, N.J.-Toledo, Ohio	Sil/Blk	SS	50's	$30
540	Lubriplate H.D.S.	Fiske Brothers Refining Co., Newark, N.J.-Toledo, Ohio	Red/Wht/Blk	SS	60's	$20
541	Lubriplate 2-C Outboard	Fiske Brothers Refining Co., Newark, N.J.-Toledo, Ohio	Red/Wht/Blk	SS	60's	$20
542	Lubriplate Super H.D.S.	Fisk Brothers Refining Co., Newark, N.J. 07105/Toledo, Oh. 43605	Sil/Ora/Yel/Red	CP	80's	$6
543	Lubriplate Super Lo.Hi.Vis.	Lubriplate Division, Fiske Brothers Refining Co., Newark, N.J./Toledo, Oh.	Wht/Gld/Red/Sil	CP	70's	$6
544	Lubriplate Super Snowmobile	Lubriplate Div. of Fisk Bros. Refining Co.,Newark N.J/Cleveland Oh. 43605	Red/Wht/Blu	CP	80's	$6
545	M & H Oil Premium Heavy Duty	Miller and Holmes Inc., St Paul, Minn.	Wht/Red/Blu	SS	60's	$75
546	M & H Oil Regular Type	Miller and Holmes Inc., St. Paul, Minn.	Wht/Yel/Blu	SS	60's	$75
547	Macmillan Ring-Free Extreme Pressure	Macmillan Petroleum Corporation, U.S.A.	Wht/Blk/Red	SS	30's	$500
548	Macmillan Ring-Free	Macmillan Petroleum Corp.,(3 street address')	Red/Blk/Wht	SS	40's	$25
549	Macmillan Ring-Free	Macmillan Petroleum Corp., Los Angeles/Chicago/New York	Wht/Red/Blk	SS	60's	$15
550	Macmillan Ring-Free New and Improved	Macmillan Petroleum Corp., Los Angeles/Chicago/New York	Wht/Red	SS	60's	$20
551	Macmillan Ring-Free 10W-30	Macmillan Petroleum Corp., Los Angeles/Chicago/New York	Wht/Red/Blk	SS	60's	$20
552	Macmillan Ring-Free Ten-Thirty	Macmillan Petroleum Corp., Los Angeles/Chicago/New York	Gld/Red/Wht	SS	60's	$20
553	Macmillan Ring-Free Outboard, Chainsaws,...	Macmillan Petroleum Corp., Los Angeles/Chicago/New York	Wht/Red/Blk	SS	60's	$20
554	Macmillan Ring-Free	Macmillan Oil Co., New York/Chicago/Los Angeles	Wht/Blu/Ora	SS	60's	$12
555	Macmillan Ring-Free 10W-30	MacMillan Ring-Free Oil Co Inc., New York/Chicago/Los Angeles	Wht/Gld/Ora/Blu	SS	60's	$20
556	Macmillan Ring-Free Outboard	MacMillan Ring-Free Oil Co Inc., New York/Chicago/Los Angeles	Wht/Ora/Blu	SS	60's	$25
557	Macmillan Ring-Free ATF	MacMillan Ring-Free Oil Co. Inc., New York/Chicago/Los Angeles	Blu/Ora/Wht	SS	60's	$20
558	Macmillan Ring Free 4 Cycle Motorcycle	Macmillan Ring-Free Oil Co. Inc., Los Angeles, Ca./N.Y.,N.Y./Eldorado, Ark.	Wht/Ora/Blu	CP	70's	$12
559	Macmillan Ring Free Multi-Service	Macmillan Ring-Free Oil Co. Inc., N.Y.,N.Y./Eldorado, Ark./Los Angeles, Ca.	Ora/Blu/Wht/Blk	CP	80's	$8
560	Macmillan Ring Free 10W-40	Macmillan Ring-Free Oil Co. Inc., Eldorado, Ark./N.Y., N.Y./Los Angeles, Ca.	Gld/Blu/Ora/Wht	CP	80's	$8

ALL PRICES LISTED IN THIS BOOK ARE FOR GRADE 9 CANS

533-535 LLL Long Life Lube: See also 405 Hudson to 414 Hudson High Detergent

 ☐ 533
 ☐ 534
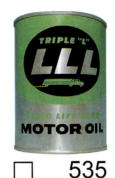 ☐ 535
 ☐ 536
 ☐ 537
 ☐ 538
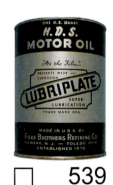 ☐ 539

 ☐ 540
 ☐ 541
 ☐ 542
 ☐ 543
 ☐ 544
 ☐ 545
 ☐ 546

 ☐5 547
 ☐5 548
 ☐5 549
 ☐5 550
 ☐5 551
 ☐ 552
 ☐ 553

 ☐ 554
 ☐ 555
 ☐ 556
 ☐ 557
 ☐ 558
 ☐ 559
 ☐ 560

#	NAME	COMPANY	COLORS	MAT.	ERA	VALUE
561	Macmillan Ring Free Xtra Heavy Duty	Macmillan Ring-Free Oil Co. Inc., N.Y.,N.Y./Eldorado, Ark./Los Angeles, Ca.	Wht/Blu/Ora/Blk	CP	80's	$8
562	Macmillan Royal Scot Heavy Duty	Royal Scot Division of Macmillan Petroleum Corp.	Grn/Yel/Red	SS	50's	$25
563	Macmillan Royal Scot Heavy Duty (.with M-12)	Macmillan Ring-Free Oil Co. Inc., New York/Chicago/Los Angeles	Grn/Red/Yel	SS	50's	$20
564	Macmillan Royal Scot 10W-30 Special	MacMillan Ring-Free Oil Co. Inc., NewYork/Chicago/Los Angeles	Gld/Red/Blk	SS	60's	$20
565	Macmillan Royal Scot ATF	MacMillan Ring-Free Oil Co. Inc., New York/Chicago/Los Angeles	Yel/Red	SS	60's	$15
566	Macmillan Royal Scot	Macmillan Ring Free Oil Co., New York/Chicago/Los Angeles	Grn/Red/Yel	CP	70's	$7
567	MacMillan Royal Scot Outboard	MacMillan Ring-Free Oil Co. Inc., NewYork/Chicago/Los Angeles	Grn/Yel/Red	CP	70's	$10
568	Macmillan Royal Scott Multi-Viscosity	Macmillan Ring-Free Oil Co. Inc., Eldorado, Ark./N.Y., N.Y./Los Angeles, Ca.	Grn/Wht/Red/Yel	CP	70's	$10
569	Macmillan Long Ranger	Macmillan Ring-Free Oil Co. Inc., N.Y.,N.Y./Eldorado, Ark./Los Angeles, Ca.	Blu/Wht/Ora	CP	70's	$12
570	Marine Special Outboard Straight Mineral Oil	Warden Oil Co., Minneapolis, Minn. (on lid of can)	Blu/Wht/Red	SS	60's	$125
571	Marine Special Outboard	Morrison Oil Co., Portland, Ore.	Grn/Wht/Red	SS	60's	$85
572	Marine Special Outboard	Pacific Petroleum Corp., Oakland, Ca.	Blu/Wht/Blk	SS	60's	$85
573	Marquette	Marquette Petroleum Products Inc., Chicago 19, Ill.	Ora/Wht/Grn	SS	50's	$175
574	Master Outboard	Kinchloe Oil Co., Dallas, Tx.	Wht/Red/Blu	SS	50's	$400
575	Maxoil Special Cylinder Lubricant	Maxoil Manufacturing Co., Amarillo, Tx.	Wht/Blu/Red	SS	60's-70's	$40
576	Midland Lanco	Midland Cooperatives Inc., Minneapolis, Mn.	Wht/Red	SS	50's	$25
577	Midland Premco Heavy Duty	Midland Cooperatives Inc., Minneapolis/Milwaukee/Mason City	Wht/Red	SS	50's	$25
578	Midland Midco	Midland Cooperatives Inc., Minneapolis/Milwaukee/Mason City	Red/Wht	SS	50's	$20
579	Midland Supreme	Midland Coop. Inc., Minneapolis, Mn.	Grn/Wht/Red	SS	50's	$20
580	Midland Golden Midco	Midland Cooperatives Inc., Minneapolis, Mn.	Wht/Grn/Red/Gld	SS	60's	$30
581	Midland Midco Heavy Duty	Midland Coop. Inc., Minneapolis, Mn.	Red/Wht/Chr	SS	60's	$20
582	Midland Golden•D	Midland Coop. Inc., Minneapolis, Mn.	Wht/Red/Gld	SS	70's	$15
583	Midland Viking Snowmobile	Midland Cooperatives Inc., Minneapolis, Minn. 55413	Red/Wht/Blk	SS	70's	$35
584	Midwest All Season Multi Grade	Midwest Oil Co., Minneapolis,Fargo, Sioux Falls	Blu/Wht/Red	SS	70's	$20
585	Midwest Hi-detergent	Midwest Oil Co., Minneapolis,Fargo, Sioux Falls	Red/Wht/Blu	SS	70's	$20
586	Midwest MOCO	Midwest Oil Co., Minneapolis,Fargo, Sioux Falls	Red/Wht/Blu	SS	60's	$20
587	Midwest Premium	Midwest Oil Co., Minneapolis,Fargo, Sioux Falls	Red/Wht/Blu	SS	60's	$20
588	Mileage	Western Oil & Fuel Co., Minneapolis 5, Mn.	Wht/Red/Blu	SS	50's	$65

ALL PRICES LISTED IN THIS BOOK ARE FOR GRADE 9 CANS

584-587 Midwest All Season to Midwest Premium: See also 3-9 Ace, 643 MOCO, 1155 Wil-Flo
588 Mileage: See also 1150 Western Mark 5, 1151 Western Mark 7

 561
 562
 563
 564
 565
 566
 567

 568
 569
 570
 571
 572
 573
 574

 575
 576
 577
 578
 579
 580
 581

 582

 583
 584
 585
 586

 587
 588

#	NAME	COMPANY	COLORS	MAT.	ERA	VALUE
589	Missile	Henley Oils, Norphlet, Ark	Grn/Blk	SS	1958	$125
590	Mobiloil "A" Gargoyle Process	A Socony Vacuum Product	Wht/Blk/Red	SS	30's	$350
591	Mobiloil "AF" Gargoyle Process	A Socony Vacuum Product	Wht/Blk/Red	SS	30's	$350
592	Mobiloil Arctic Gargoyle Process	A Socony Vacuum Product	Wht/Blk/Red	SS	30's	$350
593	Mobiloil "BB" Gargoyle Process	A Socony Vacuum Product	Wht/Blk/Red	SS	30's	$350
594	Mobiloil "A"	Product of a Socony-Vacuum Oil Company	Wht/Blk/Red	SS	30's	$300
595	Mobiloil "AF"	Product of a Socony-Vacuum Oil Company	Wht/Blk/Red	SS	30's	$300
596	Mobiloil A ("A" inside circle)	Product of a Socony-Vacuum Oil Company	Wht/Blk/Red	SS	40's	$225
597	Mobiloil Arctic ("Arctic" inside circle)	Product of a Socony-Vacuum Oil Company	Wht/Blk/Red	SS	40's	$225
598	Mobiloil Arctic Special (Arctic Special in circle)	Socony-Vacuum Oil Company, Inc.	Wht/Blk/Red	SS	40's	$200
599	Mobiloil (Gargoyle)	Socony-Vacuum Oil Company, Inc.	Wht/Blk/Red	SS	40's	$60
600	Aero Mobiloil Gold Band	Socony-Vacuum Oil Company, Inc.	Wht/Blk/Gld/Red	SS	30's	$400
601	Aero Mobiloil Gold Band (paper label)	Socony-Vacuum Oil Co., Inc.	Wht/Blk/Gld/Red	SSPL	30's	$250
602	Aero Mobiloil Gray Band	Socony-Vacuum Oil Company, Inc.	Wht/Blk/Gry/Red	SS	30's	$400
603	Aero Mobiloil Red Band	Socony-Vacuum Oil Company, Inc.	Wht/Blk/Red	SS	30's	$400
604	Mobil Mobiloil "World Famous for..."	Mobil Oil Corp., New York, N.Y.	Wht/Blu/Red	SS	60's	$12
605	Mobil Mobiloil Special	Mobil Oil Corp., New York, N.Y.	Wht/Gld/Blu/Red	SS	60's	$15
606	Mobil Super Mobiloil	Socony Mobil Oil Co. Inc., New York, N.Y.	Gld/Blu/Wht/Red	CP	70/s	$8
607	Mobil ATF for Ford Vehicles	Mobil Oil Corp., New York, N.Y. 10017	Red/Wht/Blu	CP	80's	$3
608	Mobil Universal ATF Dexron II/Ford type H	Mobil Oil Corp., New York, N.Y. 10017	Red/Wht/Blu	CP	80's	$3
609	Mobil Aero	Mobil Oil Corp., New York, N.Y.	Blu/Wht/Red	CP	70's	$10
610	Mobil ATF	Mobil Oil Corp., New York, N.Y. 10017	Blu/Wht/Red	CP	80's	$3
611	Mobil Heavy Duty (with "QUART")	Mobil Oil Corp., New York, N.Y. 10017	Blu/Wht/Red	CP	80's	$3
612	Mobil Heavy Duty (with "Quart")	Mobil Oil Corp., New York, N.Y. 10017	Blu/Wht/Red	CP	80's	$3
613	Mobiloil	Mobil Companies, New York, N.Y.	Blu/Wht/Red	CP	80's	$2
614	Mobil Mobiland	Mobil Oil Corp., New York, N.Y. 10017	Blu/Wht/Red	CP	80's	$3
615	Mobil Mobiland Net 1 Qt.	Mobil Oil Corp., New York, N.Y. 10017	Blu/Wht/Red	CP	80's	$3
616	Mobil Mobiland Net 32 Fl. oz.	Mobil Oil Corp., New York, N.Y. 10017	Blu/Wht/Red	CP	80's	$3

ALL PRICES LISTED IN THIS BOOK ARE FOR GRADE 9 CANS

 ☐ 589
 ☐ 590
 ☐ 591
 ☐ 592
 ☐ 593
 ☐5 594
 ☐5 595

 ☐ 596
 ☐5 597
 ☐ 598
 ☐5 599
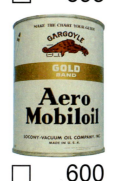 ☐ 600
 ☐ 601
 ☐ 602

 ☐5 603
 ☐5 604
 ☐4,5 605
 ☐5 606
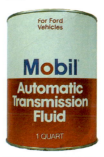 ☐ 607
 ☐ 608
 ☐ 609

 ☐ 610
 ☐ 611
 ☐ 612
 ☐4 613
 ☐ 614
 ☐ 615
 ☐ 616

#	NAME	COMPANY	COLORS	MAT.	ERA	VALUE
617	Mobil Regular Non-Detegent	Mobil Oil Corp., New York, N.Y. 10017	Blu/Sil/Red	CP	80's	$3
618	Mobiloil Special	Mobil Oil Corp., New York, N.Y.	Gld/Wht/Blu/Red	CP	70's	$4
619	Mobiloil Special 10W-30	Mobil Oil Corp., New York, N.Y.	Gld/Wht/Blu/Red	CP	80's	$4
620	Mobil Special 10W-30	Mobil Oil Corp., New York, N.Y. 10017	Gld/Wht/Blu/Red	CP	80's	$4
621	Mobil Permazone	Mobil Oil Corp., New York, N.Y.	Grn/Wht/Blu/Red	SS	70's	$20
622	Mobil Power Mower	Mobil Oil Corp., New York, N.Y.	Grn/Wht/Blu/Red	SS	70's	$35
623	Mobil Hefty 10W-30 (green version)	Mobil Chemical Co., New York, N.Y. 10017	Grn/Wht/Blu/Red	SS	70's	$50
624	Mobil Hefty (blue version)	Mobil Chemical Co., New York, N.Y. 10017	Blu/Wht/Red	SS	70's	$50
625	Mobil 1 100% Synthetic (w/ Outperforms...)	Mobil Oil Corp., New York, N.Y. 10017	Chr/Blk/Blu/Red	SS	70's	$10
626	Mobil 1 100% Synthetic (w/o Outperforms...)	Mobil Oil Corp., New York, N.Y. 10017	Chr/Blk/Blu/Red	SS	70's	$10
627	Mobil 1 "Synthesized Engine Lubricant..."	Mobil Oil Corp., New York, N.Y. 10017	Chr/Blk/Blu/Red	SS	70's	$10
628	Mobil Delvac 1100	Mobil Oil Corp., New York, N.Y. 10017	Gry/Blk/Wht/Blu	CP	70's	$5
629	Mobil Delvac 1100 Super	Mobil Oil Corp., New York, N.Y. 10017	Gry/Blk/Gld/Blu	CP	80's	$5
630	Mobil Delvac 1200	Mobil Oil Corp., New York, N.Y. 10017	Gry/Blk/Wht/Blu	CP	80's	$5
631	Mobil Delvac 1200 Super	Mobil Oil Corp., New York, N.Y. 10017	Gry/Blk/Gld/Blu	CP	80's	$5
632	Mobil Delvac 1300	Mobil Oil Corp., New York, N.Y. 10017	Gry/Blk/Wht/Blu	CP	70's	$5
633	Mobil Delvac 1300 Super	Mobil Oil Corp., New York, N.Y. 10017	Gry/Blk/Wht/Blu	CP	70's	$5
634	Mobil Delvac Super	Mobil Oil Corp., New York, N.Y. 10017	Gry/Blk/Gld/Blu	CP	70's	$5
635	Mobil H D	Mobil Oil Corp., New York, N.Y. 10017	Gld/Blu/Red	CP	80's	$3
636	Mobil HD 30	Mobil Oil Corp., New York, N.Y. 10017	Gld/Blu/Red	CP	80's	$3
637	Mobiloil Super	Mobil Oil Corp., New York, N.Y. 10017	Gld/Blu/Wht/Red	CP	80's	$3
638	Mobil Super 10W-30	Mobil Oil Corp., New York, N.Y. 10017	Gld/Blu/Red	CP	80's	$3
639	Mobil Super 10W-40	Mobil Oil Corp., New York, N.Y. 10017	Gld/Blu/Red	CP	80's	$3
640	Mobil Jet Oil II	Mobil Oil Corp., New York, N.Y.	Blu/Blk/Chr/Wht	SS	80's	$4
641	Mobil Jet Oil 254	Mobil Oil Corp., New York, N.Y.	Wht/Blk/Chr/Blu	SS	80's	$4
642	Mobil Jet Oil 291	Mobil Oil Corp., Fairfax, Va. 2037	Blk/Chr/Wht/Blu	SS	1998	$4
643	MOCO	Midwest Oil Co., Minneapolis, Fargo, Sioux Falls	Red/Wht	SS	50's	$60
644	Mohawk-Penn	Consumers Petroleum Co., Detroit, Mich.	Blk/Gld/Sil	SS	30's	$750

ALL PRICES LISTED IN THIS BOOK ARE FOR GRADE 9 CANS

643   MOCO: See also 3-9 Ace, 584-587 Midwest, 1155 Wil-Flo

#	NAME	COMPANY	COLORS	MAT.	ERA	VALUE
645	MonaMotor 100% Paraffin Base	manufactured by Barnsdall	Blu/Wht	SS	30's	$125
646	MonaMotor (w/o 100% Paraffin Base)	manufactured by Barnsdall	Blu/Wht/Blu	SS	30's	$150
647	Monarch Superior	A.E.West Petroleum Co. Inc.,Kansas City, Ks. 66115	Yel/Red/Blk/Wht	CP	80's	$5
648	Montgomery Ward 10w30 Multigrade	Montgomery Ward & Co. Inc., Chicago Il. 60671	Red/Red/Wht/Sil	CP	80's	$5
649	Montgomery Ward 10w40	Montgomery Ward & Co. Inc., Chicago Il. 60671	Gry/Ora/Wht	CP	80's	$3
650	Mother Penn (All Pennsylvania)	Dryer,Clark & Dryer Oil Co., Okla. City, Ok.	Wht/Blu/Red	SS	40's	$65
651	Mother Penn (All Pennsylvania-Premium...)	Dryer,Clark & Dryer Oil Co., Okla. City, Ok.	Wht/Blu/Red	SS	50's	$40
652	Mother Penn 10W-30	Dryer,Clark & Dryer Oil Co., Okla. City, Ok.	Blu/Gld/Red/Wht	SS	60's	$60
653	Mother Penn	Dryer,Clark & Dryer Oil Co., Okla. City, Ok. 73125	Blu/Gld/Red/Wht	CP	70's	$3
654	Motor Guard	Motor Guard Lubricants Inc., L.A., Cal. 90023	Wht/Red	CP	70's	$5
655	Motor Life Reinforced	Famous Lubricants, Inc., Chicago	Yel/Blk/Red	SS	40's	$50
656	Motor Life Detergent	Famous Lubricants, Inc., Chicago	Yel/Blk/Red	SS	60's	$30
657	Motor Seal (with Chicago address)	Bodie-Hoover Petroleum Corp., Chicago, Il.	Wht/Grn	SS	50's	$175
658	Motor Seal (with Lamont address)	Bodie Hoover Petroleum Corp., Lemont, Il. 60439	Wht/Grn	SS	60's	$150
659	Multron	Boron Oil Co., Cleveland Oh. 44115 (on bottom lid)	Wht/Blk/Blu/Chr	SS	66-75	$12
660	National Special (with Inter-State logo)	Inter-state Oil Co. Inc., Kansas City, Ks. 66119	Wht/Grn/Red/Blu	CP	80's	$5
661	National Special	Inter-state Oil Co. Inc., Kansas City, Ks. 66119	Wht/Grn/Red	CP	80's	$5
662	Neptune	Diamond Head Oil Refining Co., Kearny, N.J.	Red/Blu/Stl	SS	50's	$40
663	Nitrex	Boron Oil Co., Cleveland, Oh. 44115	Blk/Red/Blu/Wht	SS	76-81	$12
664	Nitrex Motor Oil	B.P. Oil Inc., Cleveland, Oh. 44115	Blk/Red/Blu/Wht	SS	81-89	$12
665	Nitron	Boron Oil Co., Cleveland Oh. 44115 (on bottom lid)	Wht/Blk/Red/Chr	SS	66-75	$12
666	Octron HD	Boron Oil Co., Cleveland, Oh. 44115 (on bottom lid)	Wht/Red/Blu/Gld	SS	64-65	$30
667	Oilex	Exxon Co. USA, Houston, Tx. 77001	Red/Wht	CP	1974	$4
668	Oklahoma Heavy Duty	(no company or location listed)	Wht/Red/Blu	SS	50's	$150
669	Oklahoma Super Power	Oklahoma Oil Products Corp.	Wht/Red/Blk	SS	50's	$175
670	Oklahoma Super Power High Grade	(no company or location listed)	Red/Wht/Blu	SS	50's	$175
671	Owens Pendragon	Owens-Illinois Oil Co., Bloomington, Ill.	Grn/Yel/Red	SS	40's	$400
672	Palubco	Penola Inc. (Formerly Pennsylvania Lubricating Co.), Pittsburgh, Pa.	Red/Wht	SS	30's	$40

645,646   MonaMotor: See also 103-104 Barnsadall, 105, 106 B Square, 974 Superoil, 1135 Victory

648,649   Montgomery Ward: See also 1136-1143 Vitalized to Wards

650-653   Mother Penn: See also 396, 397 Hercules

657,658   Motor Seal: See also 364 Gold Standard, 701-704 Pennstate, 705, 706 Pennsyline

659,663-666   Multron, Nitrex, Nitron, Octron HD: See also 117 Boron, 170 Cetron HD, 181 CHD, 298, 299 Facto, 365 Golden Duron, 829-833 Premex, 862, 863 QVO, 895 Sixty Two, 897-917 Sohio

660,661   National Special: See also 84 AP Type A ATF, 435-447 Inter-State

662   Neptune: See also 18 All Purpose, 225 Diamond Outboard and 2 Cycle

667-670,672   Oilex to Oklahoma Heavy Duty, Palubco: The Oklahoma brand was bought by Esso. See also 10, 11 Actol, 171 Challenge, 238-292 Esso, 684 Pate Valve Glide, 1072-1076 Uniflo

☐ 5 645   ☐ 5 646   ☐ 647   ☐ 648   ☐ 649   ☐ 5 650   ☐ 651

   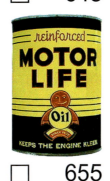 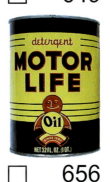  

☐ 652   ☐ 653   ☐ 654   ☐ 655   ☐ 656   ☐ 657   ☐ 658

☐ 659   ☐ 660   ☐ 661   ☐ 662   ☐ 663   ☐ 664   ☐ 665

 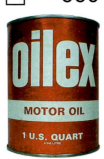    

☐ 666   ☐ 667   ☐ 668   ☐ 669   ☐ 670   ☐ 671   ☐ 672

#	NAME	COMPANY	COLORS	MAT.	ERA	VALUE
673	Pan-Am Permalube Heavy Duty	Pan-Am Southern Corp.	Wht/Blu/Red	SS	50's	$75
674	Panoco	Pan American Petroleum Corp., New Orleans, La.	Wht/Blu/Red	SS	30's	$100
675	Panoco (Pan-Am)	Pan-Am Southern Corp.	Red/Wht/Blu	SS	50's	$75
676	Paraland Stabilized	Quaker Petroleum Co., Inc.	Yel/Blk/Wht	SS	40's	$85
677	Paraland All Season 10W-30	no company or location listed (Phillips Petroleum Co.)	Blk/Gld/Wht	SS	60's	$100
678	Paraland Heavy Duty	no company or location listed (Phillips Petroleum Co.)	Blk/Yel/Wht	SS	60's	$100
679	Para Lube	Pennfield Oil Co.	Blu/Wht	SS	60's	$20
680	Para Lube 100% Paraffin Base	Pennfield Oil Co.	Blu/Wht	SS	60's	$20
681	Para Lube Heavy Duty "900"	Pennfield Oil Co.	Grn/Wht	SS	60's	$20
682	Par-O-Vis	Pennzoil Co., Oil City, Pa.	Blu/Yel	SS	50's	$35
683	Super Par-O-Vis	South Penn Oil Co., Oil City, Pa.	Yel/Blk/Red	SS	50's	$35
684	Pate Valve Glide	Pate Oil Co., Milwaukee, Wis.	Red/Wht/Blk	SS	50's	$125
685	Pemco Premium Heavy Duty	Petroleum Marketing Co., Tulsa, Ok.	Gld/Wht/Red/Blu	SS	60's	$250
686	Reverse of #685	--	Gld/Red/Blu/Wht	--	---	-----
687	Penaline	The Western Lubricating Co.	Blu/Ora/Wht	SS	30's	$60
688	Penetrex Aero Heavy Duty	Quaker Oil Corp., St. Louis, Mo.	Wht/Blu/Red	IRS2	50's	$85
689	Penetrex Outboard	Quaker Oil Corporation, St Louis, Mo. 63147	Wht/Blu/Blk	CP	70's	$12
690	Penetrex (Non Detergent in blue)	Quaker Oil Corp., St. Louis Mo. 63134	Gld/Blu/Wht	CP	60's	$5
691	Penetrex (Non Detergent in red)	Texstar Automotive Group Inc., St. Louis, Mo. 63134	Gld/Blu/Wht/Red	CP	70's	$5
692	Penetrex 10W-30 All Weather	Quaker Oil Corp., St Louis, Mo. 63147	Gld/Red/Blu/Wht	CP	70's	$5
693	Penn-Convoy	Penn Convoy Petroleum Products, Philadelphia, Pa.	Wht/Red/Blu	SS	50's	$650
694	Penndurol	J.D. Street and Co. Inc, St Louis, Mo.	Yel/Blu/Wht	SS	40's	$85
695	PennEsta	Esta Co. (no location given)	Yel/Red/Blk	SS	30's	$100
696	Pennfield	Quaker Petroleum Co. Inc.	Crm/Blu/Red	SS	30's	$250
697	Pennfield	Pennfield Oil Co.	Wht/Blu/Red	SS	60's	$150
698	Pennfield	Pennfield Oil Co.	Wht/Blu/Red	CP	70's	$25
699	Penn-Royal	Quaker Oil Corp'n., St. Louis Mo.	Grn/Blk/Wht	SS	40's	$35
700	Penn State	Penn State Oil Co., Topeka, Ks.	Blu/Wht/Red	CP	70's	$10

ALL PRICES LISTED IN THIS BOOK ARE FOR GRADE 9 CANS

673-675 Pan Am to Panoco: See also 23 American to 78 Amoco Ultimate

676-681, 696-698 Paraland Stabilized to Para Lube Heavy Duty "900", Pennfield: These brands are all related. 676 Paraland became a brand of Phillips Petroleum Co. 677 and 678 are Paraland cans sold through Phillips. 696 Pennfield was also a Quaker Petroleum Co. brand which later was produced by the Pennfield Oil Co. (697 and698), makers of 679-681 Para Lube. See also Phillips 759-822

682,683 Par-O-Vis, Super Par-O-Vis: See also 415 Hydra-Flo, 708-750 Pennzoil, 1055, 1056 Tranzport, 1175 Zoildeez, 1176 Zoilube

684 Pate Valve Glide: See also 10, 11 Actol, 171 Challenge, 238-292 Esso, 667 Oilex to 670 Oklahoma Heavy Duty, 672 Palubco, 1072-1076 Uniflo

685,686 Pemco: See also 975 Superoil

688-692, 699 Penetrex Aero to Penetrex 10W-30, Penn Royal: See also 756 Permalene 10W-30, 848-860 Quaker Maid to Quaker Maid Sno & Go

692 Penetrex 10W-30 All Weather: This can's close similarity to 756 Permalene 10W-30 All Weather suggests a close relationship between the Permalene Oil Co. and the Quaker Oil Corp./Texstar Automotive Group.

694 Penndurol: See also 404 HPX, 1168-1174 Zephyr

 673
 674
 675
 676
 677
 678
 679

 680
 681
 682
 683
 684
 685
 686

 687
 688
 689
 690
 691
 692
 693
 694

 695
 696
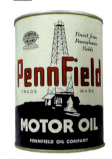 697
 698
 699
 700

#	NAME	COMPANY	COLORS	MAT.	ERA	VALUE
701	Pennstate Champion of Motor Oils	Bodie-Hoover Petroleum Corp., Chicago, Il., Warren, Pa.	Red/Blu/Wht	SS	50's	$35
702	Pennstate Heavy Duty	Bodie-Hoover Petroleum Corp., Chicago, Il.,	Blu/Red/Wht	SS	50's	$40
703	Pennstate Heavy Duty	Bodie Hoover Petroleum Corp., Lemont, Ill. 60439	Wht/Red/Blu	SS	70's	$40
704	Pennstate Heavy Duty	Bodie Hoover Petroleum Corp., Lemont, Ill. 60439	Wht/Red/Blu	CP	80's	$12
705	Pennsyline (with 35 cents)	no company or location listed (PGCOA #128, see bottom of page)	Blu/Wht/Red	SS	40's	$125
706	Pennsyline (without 35 cents)	no company or location listed (PGCOA #128, see bottom of page)	Blu/Wht/Red	SS	40's	$100
707	Pennsylvania	Industrial Oil Corp., Warren, Pa.	Yel/Blu/Wht	SS	50's	$150
708	Pennzoil (front of 709,710,711)	Pennzoil Co, Oil City, Pa.	Yel/Blk/Red	SS	30's	$----
709	Pennzoil (Economy record)	back of can 708	Yel/Blk/Red	SS	30's	$225
710	Pennzoil (New World's Record Speed)	back of can 708	Yel/Blk/Red	SS	30's	$225
711	Pennzoil (Western Air Express 35 million...)	back of can 708	Yel/Blk/Red	SS	30's	$325
712	Pennzoil (front of 713,714)	Pennzoil Co., Oil City, Pa.	Yel/Blk/Red	SS	30's	$----
713	Pennzoil (transcontinental streamliner)	back of can 712	Yel/Blk/Red	SS	30's	$325
714	Pennzoil (Western Air Express 10 Years)	back of can 712	Yel/Blk/Red	SS	30's	$275
715	Pennzoil (front of 716)	Pennzoil Co., Oil City, Pa.	Yel/Blk/Red	SS	30's	$----
716	Pennzoil (piston graphic)	back of can 715	Yel/Blk/Red	SS	30's	$125
717	Pennzoil (front of 718)	Pennzoil Co., Oil City, Pa.	Yel/Blk/Red	SS	30's	$----
718	Pennzoil (3 owls with "New Process")	back of can 717	Yel/Blk/Red	SS	30's	$65
719	Pennzoil (front of 720,721)	Pennzoil Co., Oil City, Pa.	Yel/Blk/Red	SS	30's	$----
720	Pennzoil (3 owls without "New Process")	back of can 719	Yel/Blk/Red	SS	30's	$65
721	Pennzoil (Pennzoil oval logo)	back of can 719	Yel/Blk/Red	SS	30's	$50
722	Pennzoil (front of 723)	Pennzoil Co., Oil City, Pa.	Yel/Blk/Red	SS	40's	$----
723	Pennzoil (United Air Lines plane)	back of can 722	Yel/Blk/Red	SS	40's	$60
724	Pennzoil (text in black and red stripes)	Pennzoil Co., Oil City, Pa.	Yel/Blk/Red	SS	40's	$20
725	Pennzoil (without text in black and red stripes)	Pennzoil Division, South Penn Oil Co., Oil City, Pa.	Yel/Blk/Red	SS	50's	$12
726	Pennzoil with Z-7 (red & black striped bottom)	Pennzoil Division, South Penn Oil Co., Oil City, Pa.	Yel/Blk/Red	SS	60's	$10
727	Pennzoil 10w-30 Multiple Viscosity with Z-7	Pennzoil Division, South Penn Oil Co., Oil City, Pa.	Gld/Wht/Blk/Red	SS	60's	$20
728	Pennzoil with Z-7 (plain style bell)	Pennzoil Co., Oil City, Pa. U.S.A.	Yel/Blk/Red	SS	80's	$25

ALL PRICES LISTED IN THIS BOOK ARE FOR GRADE 9 CANS

701-706 Pennstate to Pennsyline: See also 364 Gold Standard, 657, 658 Motor Seal
705,706 Pennsyline: P.G.C.O.A. #128 is listed as the Bodie-Hoover Petroleum Corp., Chicago, Ill.
708   There is a slight variation between the economy record and speed record cans.   100% Pure Pennsylvania Safe Lubrication is slightly larger on the endurance record verson than on the speed record version.
712,722 These two cans are the same except for the number of lines in the bell. 712 has six, while 722 has twelve.
708-728 Pennzoil: See also 415 Hydra-Flo, 682 Par-O-Vis, 683 Super Par-O-Vis, 729-750 Pennzoil, 1055, 1056 Tranzport, 1175 Zoildeez, 1176 Zoilube
708-723 These Pennzoil cans may look similar on their fronts but most have small differences. That is why the fronts as well as the backs are shown.
728   Pennzoil with Z-7 (plain style bell): This can was most likely made for export only.

 ☐ 701
 ☐⁵ 702
 ☐ 703
 ☐ 704
 ☐ 705
 ☐ 706
 ☐⁵ 707

 ☐ 708
 ☐⁵ 709
 ☐⁵ 710
 ☐ 711
 ☐ 712
 ☐ 713
 ☐⁵ 714

 ☐ 715
 ☐⁵ 716
 ☐ 717
 ☐⁵ 718
 ☐ 719
 ☐⁵ 720
 ☐⁵ 721

 ☐ 722
 ☐⁵ 723
 ☐⁵ 724
 ☐⁴,⁵ 725
 ☐⁴ 726
 ☐⁵ 727
 ☐ 728

67

#	NAME	COMPANY	COLORS	MAT.	ERA	VALUE
729	Pennzoil Outboard (with "Safe Lubrication")	Pennzoil Division, South Penn Oil Co., Oil City, Pa.	Yel/Blk/Red	SS	50's	$25
730	Pennzoil Outboard with Z-IP	Pennzoil Co., Oil City, Pa.	Yel/Red/Blk	SS	60's	$20
731	Pennzoil Snowmobile	Pennzoil Co., Oil City, Pa. 16301	Yel/Wht/Blk/Red	SS	70's	$20
732	Pennzoil Permanent Anti-freeze	Pennzoil Co., Oil City, Pa.	Blu/Yel/Wht/Blk	SS	70's	$30
733	Pennzoil "The Tough Film" (one quart liquid)	Pennzoil Co., Oil City, Pa.	Yel/Blk/Red	CP	70's	$4
734	Pennzoil "The Tough Film" (Net 32 FL OZ)	Pennzoil Co., Oil City, Pa. 16301	Yel/Blk/Red	CP	80's	$3
735	Pennzoil "The Tough Film" (w/Z-7)	Pennzoil Co., Oil City, Pa. 16301	Yel/Blk/Red	CP	80's	$2
736	Pennzoil 10W-30 with Z-7	Pennzoil Co., Oil City, Pa. 16301	Yel/Blk/Red	CP	70's	$4
737	Pennzoil Multi-Vis with Z-7	Pennzoil Co., Oil City, Pa. 16301	Yel/Chr/Blk/Red	CP	70's	$4
738	Pennzoil with Z-7 Multi-Vis	Pennzoil Co., Oil City, Pa. 16301	Yel/Blk/Sil/Red	CP	70's	$4
739	Pennzoil Multi-Vis 10W-30	Pennzoil Co., Oil City, Pa. 16301	Yel/Blk/Sil/Red	CP	80's	$3
740	Pennzoil Multi-Vis 10W-40	Pennzoil Co., Oil City, Pa. 16301	Yel/Blk/Sil/Red	CP	80's	$3
741	Pennzoil Long Life 15W-40	Pennzoil Co., Oil City, Pa. 16301	Yel/Red/Blk	CP	70's	$4
742	Pennzoil Multi Duty For Diesel & Gas Engines	Pennzoil Co., Oil City, Pa. 16301	Yel/Blk/Red	CP	80's	$3
743	Pennzoil P-Z-L Extended Life	Pennzoil Co., Oil City, Pa. 16301	Yel/Chr/Blk/Red	CP	70's	$5
744	Pennzoil Hydra Flo ATF (Ford on top lid)	Pennzoil Co., Oil City, Pa.	Yel/Blk/Red	CP	70's	$4
745	Pennzoil Hydra Flo ATF Dexron II	Pennzoil Co., Oil City, Pa. 16301	Yel/Blk/Red	CP	80's	$2
746	Pennzoil Hydra Flo ATF Type F	Pennzoil Co., Oil City, Pa. 16301	Yel/Red/Blk	CP	80's	$2
747	Pennzoil 2 Stroke Motorcycle	Pennzoil Co., Oil City, Pa. 16301	Sil/Yel/Red/Blk	CP	80's	$6
748	Pennzoil 4 Stroke Motorcycle	Pennzoil Co., Oil City, Pa. 16301	Sil/Yel/Red/Blk	CP	80's	$6
749	Pennzoil GT Performance	Pennzoil Co., Oil City, Pa. 16301	Sil/Yel/Red/Blk	CP	80's	$4
750	Pennzoil Racing Oil	Pennzoil Co., Oil City, Pa. 16301	Chr/Yel/Red/Blk	CP	70's	$7
751	Perfect Seal	Republic Motor Oil Co., Chicago, Ill.	Red/Yel/Blk	SS	40's	$450
752	Perfect Seal X Heavy Duty	Crystal Motor Oil Co., Chicago, Ill.	Wht/Red/Blk/Gry	SS	50's	$400
753	Perfect Seal 100% Virgin Non Detergent	Perfect Seal Oil & Chemical Co., P.O. Box 5191, Wichita, Ks.	Wht/Red/Blu	RS	60's	$85
754	Perfect Seal XHD	Perfect Seal Oil & Chemical Co., P.O. Box 5191, Wichita, Ks.	Blu/Wht/Red/Chr	RS	60's	$85
755	Perfect Seal MOS	Perfect Seal Chemical Co., Wichita, Ks.	Blu/Wht/Red/Gld	SS	50's	$10
756	Permalene 10W-30 All Weather	Permalene Oil Co., St Louis, Mo.	Gld/Red/Blu/Wht	CP	70's	$5

ALL PRICES LISTED IN THIS BOOK ARE FOR GRADE 9 CANS

729-750 Pennzoil: See also 415 Hydra-Flo, 682 Par-O-Vis, 683 Super Par-O-Vis, 708-728 Pennzoil, 1055, 1056 Tranzport, 1175 Zoildeez, 1176 Zoilube

751,752 Perfect Seal: These two cans are produced by different companies despite having the same design.

756 Permalene 10W-30 All Weather: This can's similarity in design to 692 Penetrex 10W-30 All Weather suggests a close relationship between the Permalene Oil Co. and the Quaker Oil Corp./Texstar Automotive Group. See also 688-692 Penetrex Aero to Penetrex 10W-30 All Weather, 699 Penn Royal, 848-860 Quaker Maid to Quaker Maid Sno & Go

 729
 730
 731
 732
 733
 734
 735

 736
 737
 738
 739
 740
 741
 742

 743
 744
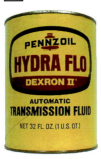 745
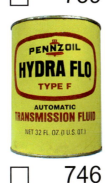 746
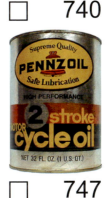 747
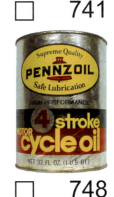 748
 749

 750
751
 752
 753
 754
755
 756

#	NAME	COMPANY	COLORS	MAT.	ERA	VALUE
757	Peter Penn	Peters Oil Co., Milwaukee	Grn/Red/Wht	SS	30's	$300
758	Petrolane LPG	Petrolane Inc., Long Beach, Ca. 90806	Grn/Ora/Wht	CP	70's	$6
759	Phillips 66 (with address on front)	Phillips Petroleum Co.	Ora/Blk	SS	1934	$125
760	Phillips 66 (with address on back)	Phillips Petroleum Co.	Ora/Blk	SS	30's	$125
761	Phillips 66 (with "The World's Finest")	Phillips Petroleum Co.	Ora/Wht/Blk	SS	1937	$75
762	Phillips 66 100% Parrafin Base	Phillips Petroleum Co.	Ora/Wht/Blk	SS	1941	$40
763	Phillips 66 (with "ONE U.S. QUART")	Phillips Petroleum Co.	Ora/Wht/Blk	SS	1948	$25
764	Phillips 66 (without registered trademark)	Phillips Petroleum Co.	Ora/Wht/Blk	SS	1950	$15
765	Phillips 66 (with registered trademark)	Phillips Petroleum Co.	Ora/Wht/Blk	SS	50's	$15
766	Phillips 66 Premium	Phillips Petroleum Co.	Mrn/Wht/Red/Blk	SS	1947	$20
767	Phillips 66 Premium Heavy Duty	Phillips Petroleum Co.	Mrn/Wht/Red/Blk	SS	1951	$20
768	Phillips 66 Trop-Artic (with palm trees)	Phillips Petroleum Co.	Wht/Grn/Ora/Blk	SS	1935	$300
769	Phillips 66 Trop-Artic (with white shield)	Phillips Petroleum Co.	Blu/Wht	SS	1938	$200
770	Phillips 66 Trop-Artic (with orange shield)	Phillips Petroleum Co.	Blu/Wht/Ora	SS	1941	$175
771	Phillips 66 Philube ATF Type A (yellow)	Phillips Petroleum Co.	Yel/Blk/Ora	SS	1950	$200
772	Phillips 66 Philube ATF Type A (Black)	Phillips Petroleum Co.	Blk/Wht/Ora	AL	1958	$150
773	Phillips 66 HDS (with large HDS)	Phillips Petroleum Co.	Crm/Blk/Wht	SS	1958	$75
774	Phillips 66 HDS	Phillips Petroleum Co., Bartlesville, Ok.	Blk/Wht	SS	1947	$75
775	Phillips 66 Unique (with orange shield)	Phillips Petroleum Co.	Grn/Wht/Red/Blk	SS	1941	$60
776	Phillips 66 Unique (with black shield)	Phillips Petroleum Co., Bartlesville, Ok.	Grn/Wht/Blk	SS	50's	$50
777	Phillips 66 Unique (with green shield)	Phillips Petroleum Co., Bartlesville, Ok.	Grn/Wht	AL	60's	$40
778	Phillips 66 Trop-Artic The All Weather...	Phillips Petroleum Co.	Gld/Wht/Blk/Red	SS	1954	$25
779	Phillips 66 Aviation (with wings)	Phillips Petroleum Co.	Blu/Red/Sil/Blk	SS	1950	$45
780	Phillips 66 Anti-freeze (with snowflakes)	Phillips Petroleum Co., Bartlesville, Ok.	Blu/Wht/Blk/Ora	SS	1953	$100
781	Phillips 66 Marine HD (with ships wheel)	Phillips Petroleum Co., Bartlesville, Ok.	Blu/Wht/Red/Blk	SS	1957	$325
782	Phillips 66 Anti-freeze (w/danger poison)	Phillips Petroleum Co., Bartlesville, Ok.	Blu/Wht/Red/Blk	SS	50's	$50
783	Phillips 66 Anti-freeze (w/o danger poison)	Phillips Petroleum Co., Bartlesville, Ok.	Blu/Wht/Red/Blk	SS	1960	$35
784	Phillips 66 Cooling System Fluid	Phillips Petroleum Co., Bartlesville, Ok.	Blu/Wht/Blk/Red	SS	1960	$35

ALL PRICES LISTED IN THIS BOOK ARE FOR GRADE 9 CANS

757 Peter Penn: See also 363 Gold-Flo
759-784 Phillips: See also 676-678 Paraland
778 Phillips 66 Trop-Artic 1954 version later was produced in an aluminum version.

 ☐ 757
 ☐ 758
 ☐5 759
 ☐5 760
 ☐5 761
 ☐5 762
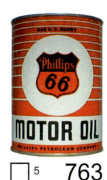 ☐5 763

 ☐5 764
 ☐ 765
 ☐5 766
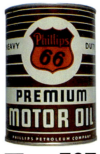 ☐5 767
 ☐5 768
 ☐5 769
 ☐5 770

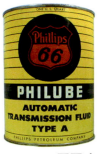 ☐ 771
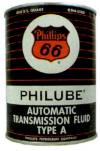 ☐ 772
 ☐ 773
 ☐ 774
 ☐ 775
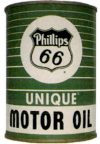 ☐ 776
 ☐ 777

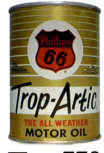 ☐5 778
 ☐ 779
 ☐4 780
 ☐ 781
 ☐ 782
 ☐1 783
 ☐ 784

#	NAME	COMPANY	COLORS	MAT.	ERA	VALUE
785	Phillips 66 Aviation	Phillips Petroleum Co., Bartlesville, Ok.	Blu/Wht/Red/Blk	AL	60's	$40
786	Phillips 66 Marine HD	Phillips Petroleum Co., Bartlesville, Ok.	Blu/Wht/Red/Blk	AL	1959	$75
787	Phillips 66 M M	Phillips Petroleum Co., Bartlesville, Ok.	Grn/Wht/Red/Blk	AL	60's	$15
788	Phillips 66 Sixty-Six	Phillips Petroleum Co., Bartlesville, Ok.	Red/Wht/Blk	AL	1959	$10
789	Phillips 66 Sixty-Six Special	Phillips Petroleum Co., Bartlesville, Ok.	Grn/Wht/Red/Blk	CP	1966	$12
790	Phillips 66 Super H D	Phillips Petroleum Co., Bartlesville, Ok.	Brn/Wht/Red/Blk	AL	60's	$25
791	Phillips 66 Trop-Artic (with "NEW")	Phillips Petroleum Co., Bartlesville, Ok.	Gld/Wht/Blk/Red	AL	1960	$40
792	Phillips 66 Trop-Artic	Phillips Petroleum Co., Bartlesville, Ok.	Gld/Wht/Blk/Red	AL	1964	$10
793	Phillips 66 Unique	Phillips Petroleum Co., Bartlesville, Ok.	Gry/Wht/Red/Blk	AL	1959	$15
794	Phillips 66 Unique (w/ "1 U.S. Quart" on front)	Phillips Petroleum Co., Bartlesville, Ok.	Gry/Wht/Blk/Red	CP	60's	$6
795	Phillips 66 Anti-freeze & Coolant	Phillips Petroleum Co., Bartlesville, Ok.	Blu/Wht/Blk/Red	SS	60's	$35
796	Phillips 66 ATF Type A Suffix A	Phillips Petroleum Co., Bartlesville, Ok.	Wht/Blk/Red	AL	1961	$40
797	Phillips 66 HDS	Phillips Petroleum Co., Bartlesville, Ok.	Red/Wht/Blk	AL	1966	$25
798	Phillips 66 ATF Dexron	Phillips Petroleum Co., Bartlesville, Ok. 74004	Blk/Wht/Red	CP	1971	$4
799	Phillips 66 ATF (F)	Phillips 66 Co., A subsidiary of Phillips Petr. Co., Bartlesville, Ok. 74004	Wht/Gry/Blk/Red	CP	1971	$4
800	Phillips 66 Anti-freeze & Coolant	Phillips Petroleum Co., Bartlesville, Ok. 74003	Wht/Blk/Blu/Red	SS	70's	$25
801	Phillips 66 Anti-freeze and Summer Coolant	Phillips Petroleum Co., Bartlesville, Ok. 74004	Wht/Blk/Blu/Red	SS	70's	$25
802	Phillips 66 Aviation Motor Oil	Phillips Petroleum Co., Bartlesville, Ok. 74004	Wht/Red/Blk/Blu	CP	80's	$8
803	Phillips 66 Aviation Oil ("Aviation" in black)	Phillips Petroleum Co., Bartlesville, Ok. 74003	Wht/Blk/Blu/Red	CP	70's	$12
804	Phillips 66 Aviation Oil ("Aviation" in red)	Phillips Petroleum Co., Bartlesville, Ok. 74003	Wht/Red/Blu/Blk	CP	70's	$12
805	Phillips 66 HDS+1	Phillips Petroleum Co., Bartlesville, Ok. 74004	Wht/Red/Blk/Pur	CP	69-70	$6
806	Phillips 66 Igloo (w / 32 oz..)	Phillips Petroleum Co., Bartlesville, Ok. 74004	Wht/Red/Blk/Chr	CP	70's	$12
807	Phillips 66 Igloo (w/o 32 oz..)	Phillips Petroleum Co., Bartlesville, Ok. 74004	Wht/Red/Blk/Chr	CP	1971	$12
808	Phillips 66 M M	Phillips Petroleum Co., Bartlesville, Ok. 74004	Wht/Grn/Blk/Red	CP	1971	$4
809	Phillips 66 Outboard	Phillips Petroleum Co., Bartlesville, Ok. 74003	Wht/Blk/Blu/Red	CP	1974	$4
810	Phillips 66 Racing	Phillips Petroleum Co., Bartlesville, Ok. 74004	Wht/Grn/Blk/Red	CP	1971	$20
811	Phillips 66 Sixty-Six	Phillips Petroleum Co., Bartlesville, Ok. 74004	Wht/Red/Blk	CP	1974	$4
812	Phillips 66 Sixty-Six Special	Phillips Petroleum Co., Bartlesville, Ok. 74003	Wht/Blk/Red/Grn	CP	70's	$8

ALL PRICES LISTED IN THIS BOOK ARE FOR GRADE 9 CANS

785-812 Phillips: See also 676-678 Paraland
785   The 4 quart version of this can lacks the stylized clouds on either side of the Phillips logo.
788   There are two styles of the 4 quart version of this can. One has smooth sides and the other has an indented ring.

 ☐ 785
 ☐ 786
 ☐ 787
 ☐ 4, 5 788
 ☐ 4 789
 ☐ 790
 ☐ 5 791

 ☐ 4, 5 792
 ☐ 793
 ☐ 794
 ☐ 795
 ☐ 796
 ☐ 797
 ☐ 798

 ☐ 799
 ☐ 800
 ☐ 801
 ☐ 802
 ☐ 4 803
 ☐ 4 804
 ☐ 805

 ☐ 806
 ☐ 807
 ☐ 808
 ☐ 809
 ☐ 810
 ☐ 4 811
 ☐ 812

#	NAME	COMPANY	COLORS	MAT.	ERA	VALUE
813	Phillips 66 Trop-Artic All Season " 1 Quart"	Phillips Petroleum Co., Bartlesville, Ok. 74003	Wht/Red/Gld/Blk	CP	1972	$4
814	Phillips 66 Trop-Artic All Season "1 US Quart"	Phillips Petroleum Co., Bartlesville, Ok. 74003	Wht/Red/Gld/Blk	CP	1968	$4
815	Phillips 66 Unique	Phillips Petroleum Co., Bartlesville, Ok. 74004	Wht/Gry/Blk/Red	CP	70's	$4
816	Phillips 66 ATF Dexron II	Phillips Petroleum Co., Bartlesville, Ok. 74004	Blk/Wht/Red	CP	70's	$4
817	Phillips 66 HDS	Phillips Petroleum Co., Bartlesville, Ok. 74004	Pur/Wht/Red/Blk	CP	80's	$4
818	Phillips 66 Super H D II	Phillips Petroleum Co., Bartlesville, Ok. 74004	Tan/Wht/Blk/Red	CP	80's	$4
819	Phillips 66 Trop-Artic All Season	Phillips Petroleum Co., Bartlesville, Ok. 74004	Gld/Blk/Wht/Red	CP	1972	$3
820	Phillips 66 Trop-Artic Fuel Economy	Phillips Petroleum Co., Bartlesville, Ok. 74004	Red/Wht/Blk	CP	1982	$3
821	Phillips 66 Trop-Artic Single Grade	Phillips Petroleum Co., Bartlesville, Ok. 74004	Sil/Blk/Wht/Red	CP	1976	$3
822	Phillips 66 X/C Aviation	Phillips Petroleum Co., Bartlesville, Ok. 74004	Blu/Wht/Red/Blk	CP	1979	$15
823	Polar anti-freeze	Warren Oil Co., Omaha, Ne.	Grn/Wht	SS	50's	$75
824	Preferred Premium	Preferred Lubricants Inc., Kansas City, Mo.	Wht/Ora/Blu	SS	40's	$40
825	Preferred Premium	no company or location listed	Wht/Red/Blu	SS	50's	$20
826	Preferred Premium	no company or location listed	Wht/Red/Blu	RS	50's	$25
827	Preferred Premium	Warren Oil Co., Omaha, Neb., 68102	Wht/Red/Blu	CP	60's	$6
828	Preferred Premium	Warren Oil Co., Omaha, Neb., 68102	Wht/Blu/Red	CP	70's	$6
829	Premex Finest Triple Grade Motor Oil	no company listed	Wht/Red/Gld	SS	64-65	$25
830	Premex Finest Triple Grade Motor Oil	Boron Oil Co., Cleveland, Oh. 44115 (on bottom lid)	Wht/Red/Chr	SS	65-67	$20
831	Premex (w/ small "1 US Quart")	Boron Oil Co., Cleveland, Oh. (on bottom lid)	Wht/Red/Chr	SS	67-70	$15
832	Premex	no company listed	Wht/Red/Chr	SS	67-70	$15
833	Premex Motor Oil (with B.P. address on front)	B.P. Oil Co., Cleveland, Oh. 44115	Wht/Red/Chr	SS	71-78	$15
834	Prestone ("Chemistry's New Discovery...")	National Carbon Co., Div. of Union Carbide and Carbon Corp., N.Y. 17, N.Y.	Blu/Gry/Red/Wht	SS	1945	$25
835	Prestone ("The New Chemical Lubricant...")	National Carbon Co., Div. of Union Carbide and Carbon Corp., N.Y. 17, N.Y.	Blu/Blu/Red/Wht	SS	1950	$20
836	Primrose 100,000 mile 35 cents	Primrose Petroleum Co., Dallas, Tx.	Blu/Wht/Yel	SS	40's	$40
837	Primrose Premium Improved	Primrose Oil Co., Dallas, Tx.	Blu/Wht/Yel	SS	50's	$35
838	Protecto ATF Type A	Petroleum Chemicals Co., Danville, Ill.	Grn/Yel/Blk/Wht	SS	50's	$30
839	Protecto Heavy Duty	Petroleum Chemicals Co., Danville, Ill.	Grn/Yel/Blk/Wht	SS	50's	$40
840	Pruitt Pennsylvania	Pruitt Petroleum Co., Philadelphia 2, Pa.	Brn/Wht	SS	50's	$40

ALL PRICES LISTED IN THIS BOOK ARE FOR GRADE 9 CANS

813-822 Phillips: See also 676-678 Paraland
823   Polar Anti-freeze: See also 102 ATF Automatic Transmission Fluid, 360-362 Gold Bond, 531 Life
829-833 Premex: See also 117 Boron, 170 Cetron HD, 181 CHD, 598, 299 Facto, 365 Golden Duron, 659 Multron, 663, 664 Nitrex, 665 Nitron, 666 Octron, 862, 863 QVO, 895 Sixty Two, 897-917 Sohio
838,839 Protecto: See also 100 Armor Heavy Duty, 101 Artic Flo, 115 Blue Star Anti-freeze, 1149 Weather Mate

 ☐ 813
 ☐⁴ 814
 ☐ 815
 ☐ 816
 ☐⁴ 817
 ☐ 818
 ☐⁴ 819

 ☐ 820
 ☐ 821
 ☐ 822
 ☐ 823
 ☐ 824
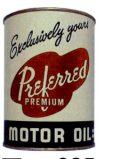 ☐ 825
 ☐ 826

 ☐ 827
 ☐ 828
 ☐ 829
 ☐⁴ 830
 ☐⁴ 831
 ☐ 832
 ☐ 833

 ☐ 834
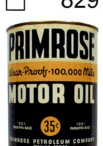 ☐ 835
 ☐⁵ 836
 ☐⁵ 837
 ☐ 838
 ☐ 839
 ☐ 840

#	NAME	COMPANY	COLORS	MAT.	ERA	VALUE
841	Quaker City (co. name & address on front)	Pennsylvania Petroleum Products Co., Phila., Pa.	Wht/Ora/Blu/Blk	SS	50's	$100
842	Quaker City ("one u.s. quart" on front)	Pennsylvania Petroleum Products Co., Phila., Pa. 19148	Wht/Ora/Blu/Blk	SS	60's	$100
843	Quaker City All Season 10W30	Pennsylvania Petroleum Products Co., Phila., Pa.	Gld/Red/Wht/Blu	SS	60's	$30
844	Quaker City All Season SAE 10W-30	Pennsylvania Petroleum Products Co., Phila., Pa.	Wht/Brn/Blk/Pur	CP	70's	$8
845	Quaker City Heavy Duty Detergent	Pennsylvania Petroleum Products Co., Phila., Pa.	Wht/Tan/Blk/Pur	CP	70's	$5
846	Quaker City Green Gear Oil	Pennsylvania Petroleum Products Co., Phila., Pa.	Wht/Grn/Blk	CP	80's	$15
847	Quaker City Select Quality Heavy Duty	Pennsylvania Petroleum Products Co., Phila., Pa.	Wht/Red/Blk/Pur	CP	80's	$5
848	Quaker Maid	Quaker Oil Corp., St. Louis, Mo.	Yel/Blk/Grn	SS	40's	$125
849	Quaker Maid	Quaker Oil Corp., St. Louis 3, Mo.	Blu/Wht/Red	SS	50's	$50
850	Quaker Maid Heavy Duty	Quaker Oil Corp., St. Louis, Mo.	Wht/Grn	SS	60's	$40
851	Quaker Maid Heavy Duty	Quaker Oil Corp., St. Louis, Mo.	Wht/Grn	CP	70's	$12
852	Quaker Maid Non Detergent	Quaker Oil Corp., St. Louis, Mo.	Wht/Grn/Red	CP	60's	$15
853	Quaker Maid Anti-freeze	Quaker Oil Corp., St. Louis, Mo.	Wht/Grn/Red	SS	60's	$25
854	Quaker Maid Anti-freeze and Summer Coolant	Quaker Oil Corp., St. Louis, Mo. 63147	Wht/Grn/Red	SS	60's	$25
855	Quaker Maid ATF Type A	Quaker Oil Corp., St. Louis, Mo.	Wht/Grn	SS	60's	$25
856	Quaker Maid Dexron II ATF	Texstar Automotive Distributing Group Inc., St Louis, Mo.	Wht/Grn/Gld	CP	70's	$10
857	QM Quaker Maid ATF	Quaker Oil Corp., St. Louis, Mo. 63147	Wht/Brn/Blk/Yel	CP	70's	$5
858	Quaker Maid Outboard	Quaker Oil Corp., St. Louis, Mo.	Grn/Wht/Blk	SS	60's	$40
859	Quaker Maid Outboard	Quaker Oil Corp., St. Louis, Mo. 63147	Wht/Grn/Blk	CP	70's	$15
860	Quaker Maid Sno & Go	Quaker Oil Corp., St. Louis, Mo. 63147	Wht/Pur/Ora/Blk	SS	70's	$25
861	Quaker Supreme ATF Suffix A Type A	Quaker Supreme Chemical Corp., Montgomery, Al.	Grn/Grn/Red	SS	60's	$25
862	QVO	Boron Oil Co., Cleveland Oh. 44115 (on bottom lid)	Pnk/Wht/Gld	SS	69-72	$20
863	QVO Motor Oil	B.P. Oil Co., Cleveland, Oh. 44115	Pnk/Wht/Gld	SS	72-75	$20
864	Real Penn	Christenson Oil Co., Portland, Ore.	Grn/Red/Wht	SS	30's	$200
865	Red Hat	Quincy Oil Co., Boston-Quincy	Red/Blk/Wht	SS	50's	$750
866	Red Seal	no company listed	Wht/Red/Blu	SS	40's	$85
867	Remco	R.E. Moore Company, Tyler, Tx	Wht/Blk/Ora	SS	30's	$25
868	Rennoco Elite 10W-40	Rennard Oil Co., St. Louis Mo. 63147	Gld/Red/Blu/Wht	CP	80's	$6

ALL PRICES LISTED IN THIS BOOK ARE FOR GRADE 9 CANS

848-860 Quaker Maid-Quaker Maid Sno & Go: See also 688-692 Penetrex Aero to Penetrex 10W30 Al Weather, 699 Penn Royal, 756 Permalene

862,863 QVO: See also 117 Boron, 170 Cetron HD, 181 CHD, 298, 299 Facto, 365 Golden Duron, 659 Multron, 663, 664 Nitrex, 665 Nitron, 666 Octron, 829-833 Premex, 895 Sixty Two, 897-917 Sohio

864   Real Penn: See also 13, 14 Aero Eastern
867   Remco: See also 530 Liberty Bond, 871 Rich-Tane

 841
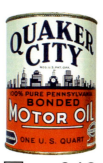 842
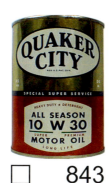 843
 844
 845
 846
 847
 848
 849
 850
 851
 852
 853
 854
 855
 856
 857
 858
 859
 860
 861

 862
 863
 864
 865
 866
 867
868

#	NAME	COMPANY	COLORS	MAT.	ERA	VALUE
869	Rev	no company or location listed	Red/Wht	SS	60's	$25
870	Rex	High Penn Oil Co. Inc., High Point, N.C.	Wht/Ora	SS	60's	$25
871	Rich-Tane	R.E. Moore Co., Tyler, Tx.	Red/Wht/Blk	SS	40's	$40
872	Rocket	Rocket Service Stations, Olean, N.Y.	Wht/Red/Blu	SS	50's	$250
873	Rotunda Permanent Anti-freeze	Ford Motor Co., Dearborn, Mich.	Red/Wht/Blu	SS	60's	$40
874	Rotunda 6000 Mile	Ford Motor Co., Detroit, Mich.	Gld/Blu/Wht/Red	SS	60's	$40
875	RRR's	Russell Oil Co., Inc., San Antonio, Tx	Grn/Wht/Blk	SS	40's	$375
876	Ser-Vis	Universal Motor Oils Co. Inc., Wichita, Ks.	Wht/Grn	SS	50's	$40
877	Servoil (without "Premium")	Petr. Prod. Corp., Milwaukee, Wis., Dist. by Parker Prod. Inc., Minneapolis	Red/Yel/Blk	SS	30's	$225
878	Servoil (with "Premium")	H.K. Stahl Co., St. Paul, Mn.	Red/Yel/Blk	SS	40's	$250
879	Shamrock 100% Pure Paraffin Base	no company or location listed	Grn/Blk/Wht	SS	40's	$75
880	Shamrock 100% Pure Pennsylvania	no company or location listed	Grn/Red/Wht	SS	40's	$75
881	Shamrock Eco Lube	Shamrock Oil & Gas Corp., Amarillo, Tx.	Wht/Grn	SS	50's	$60
882	Shamrock Motor Master	Shamrock Oil & Gas Corp., Amarillo, Tx.	Grn/Wht/Blk	SS	50's	$50
883	Shamrock Penn	Shamrock Oil & Gas Corp., Amarillo, Tx.	Red/Wht/Grn	SS	50's	$60
884	Shamrock Triple Action	Shamrock Oil & Gas Corp., Amarillo, Tx.	Grn/Yel/Wht	SS	50's	$75
885	Shamrock L-P Gas	Shamrock Oil & Gas Corp., Amarillo, Tx.	Grn/Wht/Red	SS	60's	$50
886	Shamrock Eco Lube	Shamrock Oil & Gas Corp., Amarillo, Tx.	Grn/Wht	SS	60's	$30
887	Shamrock Equa Flow 10w30	Shamrock Oil & Gas Corp.	Gld/Blk/Grn/Wht	SS	60's	$30
888	Shamrock N-D Motor Master	Shamrock Oil & Gas Corp.	Wht/Red/Grn/Blk	SS	60's	$30
889	Shamrock Triple Action	Shamrock Oil & Gas Corp.	Blk/Chr/Grn/Red	SS	60's	$30
890	Silver Bell	Tulsa Refined Oil Co., Tulsa, Ok.	Blu/Sil	SS	40's	$200
891	Site-lax	Site Oil Corp., St Louis, Mo.	Ora/Blu/Wht	SS	40's	$150
892	Site Five Star Penn All Weather 10W30	Site Oil Company	Wht/Blu/Yel/Red	SS	50's	$125
893	Site Five Star Penn 100% Pennsylvania	Site Oil Company	Red/Wht/Blu/Yel	SS	50's	$125
894	Site Supreme	Site Oil Company	Yel/Wht/Red/Blu	SS	50's	$125
895	Sixty Two	Boron Oil Co., Cleveland, Oh. 44115 (on bottom lid)	Wht/Blu/Chr	SS	67-72	$20
896	Skunk Oil Heavy Duty	Fearless Farris Stinker Stations (no location given)	Blu/Yel/Blk/Wht	SS	50's	$1250

ALL PRICES LISTED IN THIS BOOK ARE FOR GRADE 9 CANS

870 Rex: See also 398 High Penn, 1057 Triple A
871 Rich-Tane: See also 530 Liberty Bond, 867 Remco
873-874 Rotunda: See also 319-321 Fomoco, 318, 322-336 Ford
876 Ser-Vis: See also 221-224 Dezol, 458-461 Kan-O-Gold, 1083-1099 Universal
877,878 Servoil: These two cans are produced by different companies despite having the same design.
878 Servoil (with Premium): See also 12 Admiral Penn, 99 Arctic Blue Snowmobile Oil, 294 Exceloyl, 1065-1069 Trophy
879-889 Shamrock: See also 235 Eko-Lub
890 Silver Bell: See also 1058-1064 Troco
895 SixtyTwo: See also: 117 Boron, 170 Cetron HD, 181 CHD, 298, 299 Facto, 365 Golden Duron, 659 Multron, 663, 664 Nitrex, 665 Nitron, 666 Octron, 829-833 Premex, 862, 863 QVO, 897-917 Sohio

 869
 870
 871
 872
 873
 874
 875
 876
 877
 878
 879
 880
 881
 882
 883
 884
 885
 886
 887
 888
 889
 890
 891
 892
 893
894
895
 896

#	NAME	COMPANY	COLORS	MAT.	ERA	VALUE
897	Sohio Premium Quality	The Standard Oil Co. (Ohio)	Wht/Blu/Red	SS	38-40,40-46	$65
898	Sohio Premium Quality (with blue triangle)	no company or location listed	Wht/Red/Blu	SS	46-50,55-60	$30
899	Sohio Premium Quality Non Detergent	no company or location listed	Wht/Red/Blu	SS	60-62	$30
900	Sohio Non Detergent	no company or location listed	Wht/Blu/Red	SS	62-64,64-67	$25
901	Sohio HQ	The Standard Oil Co. (Ohio)	Wht/Red/Blu	SS	1947	$85
902	Sohio HQ Highest Quality	The Standard Oil Co. (Ohio)	Red/Wht/Blu	SS	47-51	$40
903	Sohio HQD (white, wiggly tail on "Q")	no company or location listed	Wht/Blu/Red	SS	51-62	$30
904	Sohio HQD (aluminum, wiggly tail on "Q")	no company or location listed	Alu/Blu/Red	AL	1960	$40
905	Sohio HQD (newer logo, straight tail on "Q")	no company or location listed	Wht/Blu/Red	SS	62-64	$30
906	Sohio HD Heavy Duty (with earlier logo)	The Standard Oil Co. (Ohio)	Wht/Red/Blu	SS	53-62	$40
907	Sohio HD Heavy Duty (with later logo)	no company or location listed	Wht/Red/Blu	SS	62-64	$40
908	Sohio HD S-3 (older 2 triangle logo)	no company or location listed	Wht/Blu/Red	SS	53-62	$50
909	Sohio HD S-3 (newer squared oval logo)	no company or location listed	Wht/Blu/Red	SS	62-64	$50
910	Sohio Premex "The New Motor Oil Discovery"	no company or location listed	Wht/Gld/Red	SS	55-62	$40
911	Sohio Premex "Finest Triple Grade MotorOil"	no company or location listed	Wht/Gld/Red/Blu	SS	62-64	$30
912	Sohio Duron	The Standard Oil Co. (Ohio)	Blk/Gld/Red/Blu	SS	62-64	$35
913	Sohio Octron HD	The Standard Oil Co. (Ohio)	Wht/Red/Gld/Blu	SS	62-64	$30
914	Sohio 7 C's Outboard	no company or location listed	Wht/Red/Blu	SS	55-62	$100
915	Sohio ATF Type "A" (with earlier logo)	no company or location listed	Wht/Red/Blu	SS	53-62	$30
916	Sohio ATF Type "A" (with later logo)	no company or location listed	Wht/Red/Blu	SS	62-64	$30
917	Super Sohio Anti-freeze	Standard Oil Co. (Ohio), Cleveland, Oh.	Blu/Gry/Wht/Red	SS	52-59	$40
918	Sooner Queen	Salyer Refining Co., Inc., Oklahoma City, Ok.	Wht/Ora/Blk	SS	40's	$1500
919	Southern Queen	Southern Oil Co. of N.C. Inc., High Point, N.C.	Wht/Grn/Red	SS	60's	$20
920	Speedol	Pennant Oil and Grease Co.	Wht/Blu/Red	SS	60's	$125
921	Stabl Flo	Chemical Research Labs, Superior, Wis.	Gld/Red/Wht/Blu	SS	1956	$50
922	StaCool	no company or location listed	Grn/Wht/Red	SS	30's-50's	$60
923	Star XXX	Star Oil Co., Tulsa, Ok.	Wht/Red/Blu	SS	30's	$125
924	Star Premium	Star Service & Petroleum Co. (no location listed)	Wht/Red/Blu	SS	40's	$50

ALL PRICES LISTED IN THIS BOOK ARE FOR GRADE 9 CANS

897-917 Sohio: See also 117 Boron, 170 Cetron HD, 181 CHD, 298, 299 Facto, 365 Golden Duron, 659 Multron, 663, 664 Nitrex, 665 Nitron, 666 Octron, 829-833 Premex, 862, 863 QVO, 895 Sixty Two

897   Sohio Premium Quality has two versions: 1938-40 has patent numbers on the side. 1940-46 version does not.

898   Sohio Premium Quality (with blue triangle) has two versions: 1946-50 "with Pentosul" 1955-60 without the "with Pentosul" text.

900   Sohio Non Detergent has two versions: 1962-64 with no company or location listed. 1964-67 listing Boron Oil Co., Cleveland, Oh.

918   Sooner Queen: See also 925, 926 Stay-Ready, 1070 Tru-Lube

 □⁵ 897
 □⁴ 898
 □ 899
 □ 900
 □⁵ 901
 □⁴,⁵ 902
 □⁴,⁵ 903

 □ 904
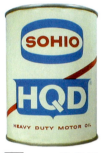 □⁴ 905
 □ 906
 □ 907
 □ 908
 □ 909
 □⁵ 910

 □⁴ 911
 □ 912
 □ 913
 □ 914
 □⁵ 915
 □ 916
 □⁴ 917

 □ 918
 □ 919
 □ 920
 □ 921
 □ 922
 □ 923
 □ 924

#	NAME	COMPANY	COLORS	MAT.	ERA	VALUE
925	Stay-Ready	Salyer Refining Co., Inc., Oklahoma City, Okla.	Yel/Blk/Red	SS	40's	$35
926	Stay-Ready ATF	Salyer Refining Co., Inc., Oklahoma City, Okla.	Blk/Wht/Red	SS	60's	$300
927	Sturdy	General Gas and Oil Co., Chicago, Il.	Wht/Red/Blk	SS	50's	$200
928	Sunland Frictionezed	Sunland Refining Corp.	Wht/Ora/Grn	SS	60's	$45
929	Sunny South	Georgia-Carolina Oil Co., Macon, Ga.	Yel/Grn/Red	SS	50's	$400
930	Sunoco Multi-Season Formula Anti-freeze	Sun Oil Co., Philadelphia, Pa. 19103	Blu/Wht/Yel/Red	SS	1964	$40
931	Sunoco Multi-Season Anti-freeze	Sun Oil Co., Philadelphia, Pa. 19103	Blu/Wht/Yel/Red	SS	1968	$40
932	Sunoco Anti-freeze and Summer Coolant	Sun Oil Co., Philadelphia, Pa. 19103	Wht/Blu/Yel/Red	SS	1972	$30
933	Sunoco DX Anti-freeze and Summer Coolant	Sun Oil Co., Philadelphia, Pa. 19103	Wht/Blu/Red/Yel	SS	1972	$25
934	Sunoco DX Anti-freeze Winter & Summer...	Sun Oil Company of Pennsylvania, Philadelphia, Pa. 19103	Wht/Blu/Red/Yel	SS	1976	$25
935	Sunoco Trans-matic Fluid	Sun Oil Co., Philadelphia, Pa.	Blu/Wht/Yel/Red	SS	1949	$40
936	Sunoco Mercury Made	Sun Oil Co., Philadelphia, Pa.	Blu/Yel/Wht	SS	37-60	$50-$30
937	Sunoco Dynalube ("Sun Oil Co." in white)	Sun Oil Co., Philadelphia, Pa.	Yel/Blu/Wht	SS	1946	$45
938	Sunoco Dynalube ("Sun Oil Co." in blue)	Sun Oil Co., Philadelphia, Pa.	Yel/Blu/Wht	SS	1946	$45
939	Sunoco Dynalube NEW	Sun Oil Co., Philadelphia, Pa.	Yel/Blu/Wht/Red	SS	1952	$40
940	Sunoco Dynalube H.D.	Sun Oil Co., Philadelphia, Pa.	Yel/Blu/Wht/Red	SS	1953	$35
941	Sunoco Dynalube ("Heavy Duty" in blue)	Sun Oil Co., Philadelphia, Pa.	Yel/Blu/Wht/Red	SS	1956	$35
942	Sunoco Dynalube ("Heavy Duty" in red)	Sun Oil Co., Philadelphia, Pa.	Yel/Blu/Wht/Red	SS	1958	$35
943	Sunoco Special High Compression	Sun Oil Co., Philadelphia, Pa.	Cop/Wht/Blu/Yel	SS	1956	$40
944	Sunoco Sun Motor Fortified	Sun Oil Co., Philadelphia, Pa.	Blu/Wht/Yel	SS	1956	$35
945	Sunoco Special	Sun Oil Co., Philadelphia, Pa.	Cop/Wht/Yel/Blu	SS	1960	$35
946	Sunoco Sun-Motor	Sun Oil Co., Philadelphia, Pa.	Blu/Sil/Yel/Red	SS	1960	$40
947	Sunoco Mercury	Sun Oil Co., Philadelphia, Pa.	Blu/Sil/Yel/Red	SS	1961	$40
948	Sunoco Improved Special 10W-40	Sun Oil Co., Philadelphia, Pa. 19103	Cop/Wht/Blu/Yel	CP	1968	$14
949	Sunoco DX Special 10W-40	Sun Oil Co., Philadelphia, Pa. 19103	Gld/Wht/Blu/Red	CP	1972	$8
950	Sunoco Sunfloot Motor Oil	Sun Oil Co., Philadelphia, Pa.	Yel/Blu/RedChr	CP	1966	$6
951	Sunoco Sunfleet Motor Oil	Sun Oil Co., Philadelphia, Pa. 19103	Yel/Blu/Red/Wht	SS	1972	$30
952	Sunoco Sunfleet Engine Oil	Sun Oil Co. of Pennsylvania	Blu/Yel/Wht/Red	CP	1972	$6

ALL PRICES LISTED IN THIS BOOK ARE FOR GRADE 9 CANS

925,926 Stay-Ready: See also 918 Sooner Queen, 1070 Tru-Lube
936 Sunoco Mercury Made: Four versions exist of this can dated 1937, 1950, 1954, and 1957

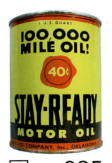 ☐ 925
 ☐ 926
 ☐ 927
 ☐ 928
 ☐ 929
 ☐ 930
 ☐ 931

 ☐ 932
 ☐ 933
 ☐ 934
 ☐5 935
 ☐5 936
 ☐5 937
 ☐5 938

 ☐5 939
 ☐5 940
 ☐5 941
 ☐5 942
 ☐5 943
 ☐5 944
 ☐5 945

 ☐5 946
 ☐ 947
 ☐ 948
 ☐ 949
 ☐ 950
☐ 951
☐ 952

#	NAME	COMPANY	COLORS	MAT.	ERA	VALUE
953	Sunoco Diamond (with small "Diamond")	Sun Oil Co., Philadelphia, Pa. 19103	Wht/Red/Yel/Blu	CP	1972	$12
954	Sunoco Diamond (with large "Diamond")	Sun Oil Company of Pennsylvania, Philadelphia, Pa. 19103	Red/Wht/Yel/Blu	CP	1976	$8
955	Sunoco DX Diamond	Sun Oil Co., Philadelphia, Pa. 19103	Red/Wht/Blu/Yel	CP	1972	$7
956	Sunoco DX Dynalube 10W-30	Sun Oil Co., Philadelphia, Pa. 19103	Yel/Wht/Blu/Red	CP	1972	$5
957	Sunoco DX Engine Oil	Manufactured for Sunmark Industries...	Blu/Wht/Yel/Red	CP	1972	$4
958	Sunoco DX Extra Heavy Duty	Sun Oil Co., Philadelphia, Pa.	Wht/Blu/Yel/Red	CP	1972	$6
959	Sunoco Sunlube (one quart)	Sun Oil Co. of Pa., Phila., Pa. 19103	Blu/Wht/Yel/Red	CP	1972	$7
960	Sunoco Sunlube (one quart .946 liter)	Sun Oil Co. of Pa., Phila., Pa. 19103	Blu/Wht/Yel/Red	CP	1976	$5
961	Sunoco DX Transmatic Fluid	Sun Oil Co., Philadelphia, Pa.	Wht/Red/Blu/Yel	CP	1972	$6
962	Sunfleet Engine Oil	Sun Oil Co., Philadelphia, Pa. 19103	Blu/Wht/Red/Blk	CP	1978	$6
963	Sunoco MPG Plus	Sun Oil Co., Philadelphia, Pa. 19103	Sil/Blk/Red/Yel	CP	1979	$8
964	Sunoco DX Dexron II ATF	Sun Refining and Marketing Co.,Phila. Pa.	Yel/Blu/Blk/Red	CP	1980	$4
965	Sunoco DX F Type ATF	Sun Refining and Marketing Co.,Phila. Pa. 19103-1699	Mrn/Wht/Yel/Red	CP	1980	$4
966	Sunoco DX F Type ATF	Sun Refining and Marketing Co.,Phila. Pa.	Yel/Blu/Red/Wht	CP	1982	$4
967	Sunoco DX Diesel Super C 15W40	Sun Refining and Marketing Co.,Phila. Pa.	Gry/Wht/Blu/Yel	CP	1980	$4
968	Sunoco DX Diesel Super C SAE 30	Sun Refining and Marketing Co.,Phila. Pa. 19103	Gry/Wht/Blu/Red	CP	1980	$4
969	Sunoco GT High Performance 20W50	Sun Refining and Marketing Co., Philadelphia, Pa. 19103-1699	Red/Yel/Wht/Blk	CP	1980	$6
970	Sunoco DX HD High Detergent Single Grade	Sun Refining and Marketing Co.,Phila. Pa.	Blu/Wht/Yel/Red	CP	1980	$4
971	Sunoco Plus 4 Cylinder Engines	Sun Refining and Marketing Co., Philadelphia, Pa. 19103-1699	Sil/Yel/Blk/Red	CP	80-84	$6
972	Sunoco DX Special 10W40 SF	Sun Refining and Marketing Co., Philadelphia, Pa. 19103-1699	Cop/Blk/Red/Yel	CP	1980	$4
973	Sunoco DX Ultra 5W30 SF	Sun Refining and Marketing Co.,Phila. Pa.	Sil/Red/Yel/Wht	CP	1984	$4
974	Superoil	Bareco Oil Co., Tulsa, Ok.	Yel/Blk/Wht	SS	40's	$65
975	Superoil	Petroleum Marketing Corp., Tulsa, Ok.	Yel/Blk/Wht	SS	30's	$65
976	Super Penn	Smith Oil & Refining Co., Rockford, Il.	Yel/Blk/Red	SS	30's	$85
977	Super Penn Triple Film	Smith Oil & Refining Co., Rockford, Il.	Yel/Blk/Red	SS	50's	$60
978	Super Power	Warren Oil Company of Ohio	Sil/Grn/Red/Gld	SS	30's	$50
979	Super Power	Warren Oil Company	Wht/Grn/Red	SS	50's	$35
980	Swift	Oscar Bryant, Hollis, Ok.	Wht/Red/Grn	SS	40's	$8

ALL PRICES LISTED IN THIS BOOK ARE FOR GRADE 9 CANS

974   Superoil: See also 103-104 Barnsdall, 105, 106 B Square, 645, 646 Monamotor, 1135 Victory
975   Superoil: See also 685, 686 Pemco
978,979 Super Power: See also 358, 359 Gold Bond
980   Swift: See also 300 Falcon

 953	 954	 955	 956	 957	 958	 959
 960	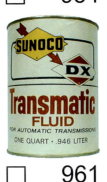 961	 962	 963	 964	 965	 966
 967	 968	 969	 970	 971	 972	 973
 974	 975	 976	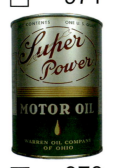 977	 978	 979	 980

#	NAME	COMPANY	COLORS	MAT.	ERA	VALUE
981	New Texaco Airplane (w/ planes and hanger)	The Texas Co. (no address listed)	Wht/Grn/Blk/Red	SS	40's	$1250
982	Texaco Aircraft (w/wings, text in green)	The Texas Co. (no address listed)	Wht/Red/Grn	SS	40's	$60
983	Texaco Aircraft (w/wings, text in white)	The Texas Co. (no address listed)	Wht/Red/Grn	SS	50's	$50
984	Texaco Aircraft (w/large arrow & round logo)	Texaco Inc.,(no address listed)	Wht/Red/Grn	SS	12-61	$30
985	Texaco Aircraft (w/small arrow & round logo)	Texaco Inc., (no address listed)	Wht/Red/Grn	SS	11-64	$25
986	Texaco Aircraft (w/logo below text)	Texaco Inc., New York, N.Y. 10017	Wht/Red/Grn	SS	5-68	$15
987	Texaco Aircraft (w/logo above text)	Texaco Inc., White Plains, N.Y. 10650	Wht/Red/Grn	SS	7-78	$10
988	Texaco Aircraft Premium A-D	Texaco Inc., New York, N.Y.	Chr/Red/Blk/Wht	SS	11-66	$25
989	Texaco Aircraft Premium A D	Texaco Inc., New York, N.Y. 10017	Gld/Red/Blk/Wht	SS	5-68	$20
990	Texaco Aircraft Premium A D	Texaco Inc., White Plains, N.Y. 10650	Gld/Red/Blk/Wht	SS	7-79	$15
991	Texaco D 303 HD	The Texas Co. (no address listed)	Blk/Wht/Red/Grn	SS	3-56	$50
992	Texaco D 303 HD	Texaco Inc. (no address listed)	Grn/Wht/Red	SS	5-59	$45
993	Texaco Heavy Duty	Texaco Inc., New York, N.Y. 10017	Wht/Red/Grn	SS	6-77	$8
994	Texaco Improved (The Texas Company)	The Texas Co. (no address listed)	Red/Wht/Grn	SS	40's	$20
995	Texaco Improved (Texaco Inc.)	Texaco Inc. (no address listed)	Red/Wht/Grn	SS	50's	$15
996	Texaco Insulated	The Texas Co. (no address listed)	Red/Wht/Grn	SS	40's	$20
997	Texaco Insulated API ML & MM	The Texas Co. (no address listed)	Red/Wht/Grn	SS	50's	$15
998	Texaco Marine "High Grade Uniform.."	The Texas Co. USA (no address listed)	Wht/Grn/Blk/Red	SS	30's	$250
999	Texaco Marine (w/o "High Grade..")	The Texas Co. USA (no address listed)	Wht/Grn/Blk/Red	SS	40's	$150
1000	Texaco Marine (with straight "Texaco")	The Texas Co. (no address listed)	Wht/Grn/Blk/Red	SS	40's	$150
1001	Texaco Motor Oil (black outlined "T")	The Texas Co., USA	Red/Wht/Blk/Grn	SS	30's	$40
1002	Texaco Motor Oil	Texaco Inc. (no address listed)	Red/Wht/Grn	SS	5-62	$10
1003	Texaco Motor Oil	Texaco Inc. (no address listed)	Wht/Red/Grn	SS	11-62	$8
1004	Texaco Motor Oil	Texaco Inc., New York, N.Y. 10017	Wht/Red/Grn	SS	11-68	$6
1005	Texaco Motor Oil	Texaco Inc., White Plains, N.Y. 10650	Wht/Red/Grn	SS	7-79	$5
1006	Texaco Motor Oil	Texaco Inc., White Plains, N.Y. 10650	Wht/Red/Grn	CP	1-82	$3
1007	Texaco New Motor Oil (green text)	The Texas Co. (no address listed)	Red/Wht/Grn	SS	30's	$40
1008	Texaco New Motor Oil (black text)	The Texas Co. (no address listed)	Red/Wht/Blk	SS	30's	$40

ALL PRICES LISTED IN THIS BOOK ARE FOR GRADE 9 CANS

982,983 Texaco Aircraft (with wings): The Texas Company, Made in U.S.A., One US Quart and 0.946 Litre are in green on 982 while it is in white on 983.
988   There is a version of this can dated 2-65 with the same front but a different back.

 981
 982
 983
 984
 985
 986
 987

 988
 989
 990
 991
 992
 993 994

 995
 996
 997
 998
 999 1000
 1001

 1002

 1003

 1004
 1005
 1006
 1007 1008

#	NAME	COMPANY	COLORS	MAT.	ERA	VALUE
1009	Texaco Outboard (with ships)	The Texas Co. (no address listed)	Wht/Grn/Blk/Red	SS	40's	$250
1010	Texaco Outboard SAE 30	Texaco Inc., New York, N.Y.	Wht/Grn/Red	SS	5-66	$25
1011	Texaco Outboard With Royal Guard SAE 30	Texaco Inc., New York, N.Y. 10017	Wht/Pur/Red	SS	11-68	$20
1012	Texaco Outboard 50-1 SAE 20	Texaco Inc., New York, N.Y. 10017	Wht/Blu/Red	SS	1-73	$15
1013	Texaco Permanent Type Anti-freeze	The Texas Co. (no address listed)	Wht/Red/Grn	SS	30's	$50
1014	Texaco PT Anti-freeze Permanent Type	The Texas Co., New York, 17, N.Y.	Wht/Red/Grn	SS	40's	$40
1015	Texaco PT Anti-freeze "One Fill Protects…"	The Texas Co., New York, 17, N.Y.	Wht/Red/Grn	SS	40's	$40
1016	Texaco Premium Type Anti-freeze	The Texas Co., New York, 17, N.Y.	Gld/Wht/Red/Grn	SS	3-58	$35
1017	Texaco Anti-freeze Permanent Type	Texaco Inc., New York, 17, N.Y.	Gld/Wht/Red/Grn	SS	4-62	$35
1018	Texaco Anti-freeze Permanent Type	Texaco Inc., New York, N.Y.	Gld/Wht/Red/Grn	SS	3-66	$25
1019	Texaco Anti-freeze Coolant	Texaco Inc., New York, N.Y. 10017	Gld/Wht/Red/Blk	SS	4-72	$15
1020	Texaco Sato 7730	Texaco Inc., New York, N.Y. 10017	Grn/Wht/Red	SS	1-69	$50
1021	Texaco Starjet-5	Texaco Inc., New York, N.Y. 10017	Red/Chr/Blk/Wht	SS	10-71	$75
1022	Texaco Starjet-5	Texaco Inc., New York, N.Y. 10017	Red/Wht/Blk	SS	9-76	$40
1023	Texaco Texamatic Fluid Type A	The Texas Company	Wht/Red/Grn	SS	50's	$30
1024	Texaco Texamatic Fluid (Made in USA)	Texaco Inc. (no address listed)	Wht/Grn/Red	SS	1-60	$20
1025	Texaco Texamatic Fluid (N.Y. 17, N.Y.)	Texaco Inc., New York 17, N.Y.	Wht/Grn/Red	SS	12-61	$20
1026	Texaco Texamatic Fluid Type A	Texaco Inc., New York, N.Y.	Wht/Grn/Red	SS	5-66	$15
1027	Texaco Texamatic Fluid Dexron (B-10101)	Texaco Inc., New York, N.Y. 10017	Wht/Grn/Red	SS	11-68	$12
1028	Texaco Texamatic Fluid Dexron	Texaco Inc., New York, N.Y. 10017	Wht/Grn/Red	SS	7-72	$12
1029	Texaco Texamatic Fluid Dexron II	Texaco Inc., White Plains, N.Y. 10650	Wht/Grn/Red	SS	7-79	$10
1030	Texaco Texamatic Fluid Dexron II	Texaco Inc., White Plains, N.Y. 10650	Wht/Grn/Red	CP	9-82	$6
1031	Texaco Texamatic Type F ATF	Texaco Inc., New York, N.Y. 10017	Grn/Wht/Red	CP	7-73	$8
1032	Texaco Texamatic Type F ATF	Texaco Inc., White Plains, N.Y. 10650	Grn/Wht/Red	SS	7-80	$8
1033	Texaco Texamatic Type F ATF	Texaco Inc., White Plains, N.Y. 10650	Grn/Wht/Red	CP	6-83	$6
1034	Texaco Turbine Oil 15	Texaco Inc.	Gld/Red/Blk/Wht	SS	4-60	$40
1035	Texaco Turbine Oil 35	Texaco Inc.	Wht/Gld/Blk/Red	SS	4-60	$40
1036	Texaco Ursa E-D	Texaco Inc., New York, N.Y.	Wht/Blu	SS	10-67	$15

ALL PRICES LISTED IN THIS BOOK ARE FOR GRADE 9 CANS

1016 Texaco PT Anti-freeze Note: There is a variation of this can dated 2-59 with the same front but different text on the back.

 ☐ 1009
 ☐ 1010
 ☐ 1011
 ☐ 1012
 ☐ 1013
 ☐⁴ 1014
 ☐ 1015

 ☐ 1016
 ☐ 1017
 ☐ 1018
 ☐⁴ 1019
 ☐ 1020
 ☐ 1021
 ☐ 1022

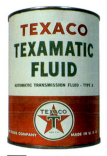 ☐ 1023
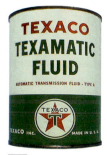 ☐ 1024
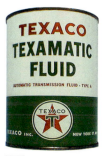 ☐ 1025
 ☐ 1026
 ☐ 1027
 ☐ 1028
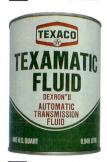 ☐ 1029

 ☐ 1030
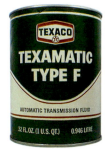 ☐ 1031
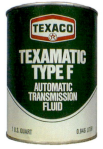 ☐ 1032
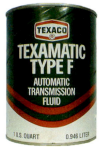 ☐ 1033
 ☐ 1034
 ☐ 1035
 ☐ 1036

#	NAME	COMPANY	COLORS	MAT.	ERA	VALUE
1037	Texaco Ursa ED	Texaco Inc., New York, N.Y. 10017	Wht/Red	SS	8-68	$15
1038	Texaco Ursa ED	Texaco Inc., White Plains, N.Y. 10650	Wht/Red	SS	7-79	$10
1039	Texaco Ursa LA-3	Texaco Inc., New York, N.Y. 10017	Grn/Wht	SS	2-72	$10
1040	Texaco Ursa LA-3	Texaco Inc., New York, N.Y. 10017	Grn/Wht	PL	2-72	$25
1041	Texaco Ursa S1	Texaco Inc. (no address listed)	Wht/Gld	SS	10-61	$20
1042	Texaco Ursa S1	Texaco Inc., New York, N.Y. 10017	Wht/Red	SS	2-68	$20
1043	Texaco Ursa S3	Texaco Inc. (no address listed)	Wht/Grn	SS	10-61	$20
1044	Texaco Ursa S3 Motor Oil	Texaco Inc., New York, N.Y. 10017	Wht/Grn	SS	8-68	$20
1045	Texaco Ursa Super Plus	Texaco Inc., White Plains, N.Y. 10650	Grn/Wht	SS	7-80	$10
1046	Texaco Ursa Super Plus	Texaco Inc., White Plains, N.Y. 10650	Grn/Wht	CP	10-82	$5
1047	Texaco Ursa Super-3 (Super 3 in black strip)	Texaco Inc., New York, N.Y. 10017	Wht/Red/Blk	SS	7-72	$30
1048	Texaco Ursa Super-3	Texaco Inc., New York, N.Y. 10017	Wht/Blk/Red	SS	1-77	$8
1049	Texaco Ursatex	Texaco Inc., New York, N.Y. 10017	Wht/Blu	SS	8-68	$20
1050	Texaco Ursatex	Texaco Inc., White Plains, N.Y. 10650	Wht/Blu	SS	7-79	$10
1051	Thoni's High Grade	Thoni's Oil Co., Nashville, Tn.	Blu/Wht/Ora	SS	30's	$60
1052	Tiopet	Tiona Petroleum Co., Philadelphia, Pa.	Red/Blu/Wht	SS	40's	$450
1053	Tiopet	Tiona Petroleum Co., Philadelphia, Pa.	Red/Wht/Blu	SS	60's	$350
1054	Tip Top Penn	Product of Valvoline Oil Co.	Red/Wht	SS	40's	$50
1055	Tranzport (curved text on bottom)	Tranzport Oil Division, Pennzoil Co., Oil City, Pa.	Wht/Blu	SS	30's	$50
1056	Tranzport (horizontal text on bottom)	Pennzoil Co., Oil City, Pa.	Yel/Blk	SS	60's	$15
1057	Triple A	High Penn Oil Co. Inc., High Point, N.C.	Wht/Blu	SS	60's	$15
1058	Troco	Tulsa Refined Oil Co., Tulsa, Ok.	Ora/Blk/Wht	SS	50's	$30
1059	Troco	Troco Oil Co., Tulsa, Ok.	Ora/Blk/Sil	CP	60's	$10
1060	Troco Extra Heavy Duty (without round logo)	Troco Oil Co., Tulsa, Ok. 74101	Org/Wht/Blk/Blu	CP	80's	$8
1061	Troco Extra Heavy Duty (with round logo)	Troco Oil Co., Tulsa, Ok. 74101	Ora/Wht/Blk/Blu	CP	80's	$10
1062	Troco Diesel Supreme (yellow)	Troco Oil Co., Tulsa, Ok. 74101	Wht/Yel/Blk	PL	70's	$20
1063	Troco Diesel Supreme 15W-40	Troco Oil Co., Tulsa, Ok. 74101	Blk/Gld/Wht/Red	CP	80's	$6
1064	Troco Diesel Supreme	Troco Oil Co., Tulsa, Ok. 74101	Blk/Gld/Wht/Red	CP	80's	$6

ALL PRICES LISTED IN THIS BOOK ARE FOR GRADE 9 CANS

1054		Tip Top Penn: See also 107 Beaver Penn, 337 Fort Pitt, 339-341 Freedom, 350-352 Galena, 1100-1134 Valvoline
1055,1056		Tranzport: See also 415 Hydra-Flo, 682 Par-O-Vis, 683 Super Par-O-Vis, 708-750 Pennzoil, 1175 Zoildeez, 1176 Zoilube
1056		Tranzport: A second variation exists with Pennzoil Division, South Penn Oil Co., Oil City, Pa. as the address.
1057		Triple A: See also 398 High Penn, 870 Rex
1058-1064		Troco: See also 892 Silver Bell

 1037
 1038
 1039
 1040
 1041
 1042
 1043

 1044
 1045
 1046
 1047
 1048
 1049
 1050

 1051
 1052
 1053
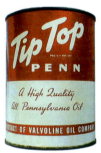 1054
 1055
 1056
 1057

 1058
 1059
 1060
 1061
 1062
 1063
 1064

#	NAME	COMPANY	COLORS	MAT.	ERA	VALUE
1065	Trophy 40 below	H.K. Stahl Co., St. Paul, Mn.	Blu/Wht/Yel/Blk	SS	30's	$300
1066	Trophy 100% Pure Paraffin	H.K. Stahl Co., St. Paul, Mn.	Blu/Wht/Red	SS	40's	$65
1067	Trophy H.D.	H.K. Stahl Co., St. Paul, Mn.	Wht/Blu/Red	SS	50's	$50
1068	Trophy EDO	Metalcote Grease & Oil Co., GOA Corp., St Paul, Mn. 55102	Blu/Wht/Gld	SS	70's	$30
1069	Trophy Non Detergent	Metalcote Grease & Oil Co., GOA Corp., St Paul, Mn. 55102	Red/Wht/Gld/Blk	SS	70's	$30
1070	Tru-Lube	Salyer Oil Co., Oklahoma City	Yel/Wht/Blk	SS	30's	$150
1071	Tulane	Benz Oil Inc., Milwaukee, Wis. 53209	Red/Grn/Wht	SS	60's	$175
1072	Uniflo Low Consumption	Penola Inc., Pittsburgh, Pa.	Wht/Red/Blu	SS	1934	$100
1073	Uniflo Low Consumption	(same as above w/o Penola, Pittsburgh)	Wht/Red/Blu	SS	1934	$100
1074	Uniflo Winter	Pennsylvania Lubricating Co., Pittsburgh Pa.	Wht/Red/Blu	SS	1934	$125
1075	Uniflo	Skelly Oil Co. Distributors	Wht/Red/Blu	SS	30's	$35
1076	Uniflo	Skelly Oil Co. Distributors (on lid)	Wht/Red/Blu	SS	30's	$25
1077	Uni-Penn	United Petroleum Corporation, Omaha	Grn/Gld/Blk	SS	40's	$40
1078	United All-Weather	United Petroleum Corporation, Omaha, Ne.	Wht/Blu/Red	SS	60's	$35
1079	United D-300 Heavy Duty	United Petroleum Corporation, Omaha, Ne.	Wht/Blu/Red	SS	60's	$35
1080	United D-300 Heavy Duty (in jagged oval)	United Petroleum Corporation, Omaha, Ne.	Wht/Blu/Red	SS	60's	$35
1081	United Unilene	United Petroleum Corporation, Omaha, Ne.	Wht/Blu/Red	SS	60's	$35
1082	United	United Petroleum Corporation, Omaha, Ne.	Wht/Blu/Red	CP	70's	$10
1083	Universal Bonded (with globe)	Universal Motor Oils Co., Wichita, Ks.	Sil/Blu	SS	30's	$300
1084	Universal Hi Viscosity Index Bonded	Universal Motor Oils Co. Inc., Wichita, Ks.	Blu/Wht	SS	60's	$30
1085	Universal Hi Viscosity Index Non Det.	Universal Motor Oils Co. Inc., Wichita, Ks.	Blu/Wht	RS	60's	$25
1086	Universal Super Outboard	Universal Motor Oils Co. Inc., Wichita, Ks.	Blu/Chr	RS	60's	$40
1087	Universal HVI Non-Detergent	Universal Motor Oils Co. Inc., Wichita, Ks.	Wht/Blu/Gld	RS	70's	$15
1088	Universal HVI Non-Detergent	Universal Motor Oils Co. Inc., Wichita, Ks.	Wht/Blu/Gld/Chr	RS	70's	$15
1089	Universal ATF Dexron	Universal Motor Oils Co. Inc., Wichita, Ks. 67202	Blu/Wht/Gld/Red	RS	70's	$20
1090	Universal Extra Heavy Duty	Universal Motor Oils Co. Inc., Wichita, Ks.	Wht/Blu/Gld/Red	RS	70's	$20
1091	Universal Super Extra Heavy Duty	Universal Motor Oils Co. Inc., Wichita, Ks.	Wht/Blu/Gld/Red	RS	70's	$20
1092	Universal Series III	Universal Motor Oils Co. Inc., Wichita, Ks.	Wht/Blu/Gld/Red	RS	70's	$20

ALL PRICES LISTED IN THIS BOOK ARE FOR GRADE 9 CANS

1065-1069	Trophy: See also 12 Admiral Penn, 99 Arctic Blue Snowmobile Oil, 294 Exceloyl, 878 Servoil #2
1065-1069	Originally a brand of the H.K. Stahl Co., Trophy became a brand of the Metalcote Grease & Oil Co. along with 99 Arctic Blue Snowmobile Oil
1070	Tru-Lube: See also 918 Sooner Queen, 925, 926 Stay-Ready
1071	Tulane: has a variation with no address and a white painted seam
1072-1076	Uniflo: See also 10, 11 Actol, 171 Challenge, 238-292 Esso, 667 Oilex to 670 Oklahoma Heavy Duty, 672 Palubco, 684 Pate Valve Glide
1083-1092	Universal: See also 221-224 Dezol, 458-461 Kan-O-Gold, 876 Ser-Vis, 1093-1099 Universal

 1065
 1066
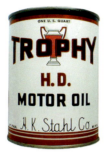 1067
 1068
 1069
 1070
 1071

 ^{5} 1072
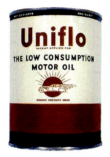 1073
 ^{5} 1074
 ^{5} 1075
 ^{5} 1076
 1077
 1078

 1079
 1080
 1081
 1082
 ^{5} 1083
 1084
 1085

 1086
 1087
 1088
 1089
 1090
 1091
 1092

#	NAME	COMPANY	COLORS	MAT.	ERA	VALUE
1093	Universal 10W-30 All Season	Universal Motor Oils Co. Inc., Wichita, Ks.	Wht/Blu/Gld/Red	RS	70's	$20
1094	Universal	Universal Motor Oils Co. Inc., Wichita, Ks. 67219	Ora/Blu/Wht	CP	70's	$8
1095	Universal ATF	Universal Motor Oils Co. Inc., Wichita, Ks. 67219	Red/Wht/Gld/Blu	CP	80's	$8
1096	Universal Dezol	Universal Motor Oils Co. Inc., Wichita, Ks. 67219	Brn/Wht/Gld/Blu	CP	80's	$8
1097	Universal HVI Non-Detergent	Universal Motor Oils Co. Inc., Wichita, Ks. 67219	Grn/Wht/Blu/Red	CP	80's	$8
1098	Universal Series III	Universal Motor Oils Co. Inc., Wichita, Ks. 67219	Yel/Wht/Blk/Red	CP	80's	$8
1099	Universal Super Extra Heavy Duty	Universal Motor Oils Co., Wichita, Ks.	Blu/Wht/Gld	CP	80's	$8
1100	Valvoline 35 cents per quart	Valvoline Oil Co. (12 principal offices listed)	Grn/Wht/Blk	SS	30's	$100
1101	Valvoline The Original... (with round "O")	Valvoline Oil Co., Cincinnati, Oh.	Grn/Wht/Red	SS	30's	$35
1102	Valvoline The Original... (with elongated "O")	Freedom-Valvoline Oil Co., Freedom, Pa.	Grn/Wht/Red	SS	40's	$20
1103	Valvoline "The World's First Motor Oil"	Freedom-Valvoline Oil Co., Freedom, Pa.	Grn/Wht/Red	SS	50's	$15
1104	Valvoline "The World's First Motor Oil"	Valvoline Oil Co., Division of Ashland Oil and Refining Co., Freedom, Pa.	Grn/Wht/Red	SS	50's	$15
1105	Valvomatic Fluid	Valvoline Oil Co., Freedom, Pa., Division of Ashland Oil & Refining Co.	Grn/Wht/Red	SS	50's	$25
1106	Valvoline F.C. Heavy Duty	Freedom-Valvoline Oil Co., Freedom, Pa.	Grn/Yel/Wht	SS	1951	$40
1107	Valvoline All Climate Heavy Duty	Valvoline Oil Co., Division of Ashland Oil and Refining Co., Freedom, Pa.	Gld/Wht/Grn	SS	60's	$25
1108	Valvoline (without Net 32 Fl. Oz...)	Valvoline Oil Co., Division of Ashland Oil and Refining Co., Freedom, Pa.	Wht/Red/Blu	SS	60's	$12
1109	Valvoline Permanent Anti-freeze	Ashland Oil and Refining Co., Ashland, Ky.	Wht/Red/Blu	SS	60's	$40
1110	Valvoline Super Outboard	Valvoline Oil Co., Division of Ashland Oil and Refining Co., Freedom, Pa.	Wht/Red/Blu/Gld	SS	60's	$35
1111	Valvoline XLD	Valvoline Oil Co., Division of Ashland Oil and Refining Co., Freedom, Pa.	Wht/Blu/Red	SS	60's	$25
1112	Valvomatic ATF	Valvoline Oil Co., Division of Ashland Oil, Ashland, Ky. 41101	Wht/Blu/Red	CP	70's	$6
1113	Valvoline Racing	Valvoline Oil Co., Division of Ashland Oil, Ashland, Ky. 41101	Wht/Red/Blu/Blk	CP	70's	$8
1114	Valvoline Snowmobile	Valvoline Oil Co., Division of Ashland Oil, Ashland, Ky. 41101	Wht/Blu/Red	CP	70's	$12
1115	Valvoline Motor Oil (with Net 32 Fl. Oz...)	Valvoline Oil Co., Division of Ashland Oil, Ashland, Ky. 41101	Wht/Red/Blu/Blk	CP	80's	$3
1116	Valvoline XLD	Valvoline Oil Co., Ashland, Ky.	Gld/Wht/Blu/Red	CP	80's	$4
1117	Valvoline All Climate Heavy Duty	Valvoline Oil Co., Division of Ashland Oil, Ashland, Ky. 41101	Wht/Red/Blu/Gld	CP	80's	$4
1118	Valvoline All Climate HD 10W-20W-40	Valvoline Oil Co., Division of Ashland Oil, Ashland, Ky. 41101	Wht/Red/Blu/Gld	CP	80's	$4
1119	Valvoline All Climate 5W-30	Valvoline Oil Co., Ashland, Ky.	Wht/Blu/Red/Gld	CP	80's	$3
1120	Valvoline All Climate 10W-40	Valvoline Oil Co., Division of Ashland Oil Inc. Ashland, Ky. 41114	Wht/Blu/Red/Gld	CP	80's	$3

ALL PRICES LISTED IN THIS BOOK ARE FOR GRADE 9 CANS

1093-1099   Universal: See also 221-224 Dezol, 458-461 Kan-O-Gold, 876 Ser-Vis, 1083-1092 Universal
1100-1120   Valvoline: See also 107 Beaver Penn, 337 Fort Pitt, 339-341 Freedom, 350-352 Galena, 1054 Tip Top Penn, 1121-1134 Valvoline
1103   This can has less green above "Valvoline" and lists 18 branches on the back
1104   This can has more green above "Valvoline" and has "Distributed by Pan-Am Southern Corporation" on the back.

☐ 1093 ☐ 1094 ☐ 1095 ☐ 1096 ☐ 1097 ☐ 1098 ☐ 1099

  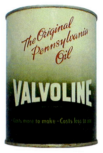 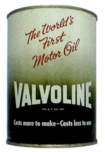 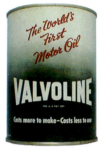 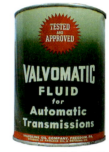 

☐⁵ 1100 ☐⁵ 1101 ☐ 1102 ☐⁵ 1103 ☐ 1104 ☐ 1105 ☐ 1106

☐ 1107 ☐ 1108 ☐ 1109 ☐ 1110 ☐ 1111 ☐ 1112 ☐ 1113

☐ 1114 ☐ 1115 ☐ 1116 ☐ 1117 ☐ 1118 ☐ 1119 ☐ 1120

#	NAME	COMPANY	COLORS	MAT.	ERA	VALUE
1121	Valvoline All Climate 20W-50	Valvoline Oil Co., Division of Ashland Oil Inc. Ashland, Ky. 41114	Wht/Blu/Red/Gld	CP	80's	$3
1122	Valvoline All-Fleet Plus	Valvoline Oil Co., Division of Ashland Oil, Ashland, Ky. 41101	Wht/Red/Blu	CP	80's	$4
1123	Valvoline ATF Dexron II	Valvoline Oil Co., Division of Ashland Oil, Ashland, Ky. 41101	Wht/Blu/Red	CP	80's	$3
1124	Valvoline ATF Type FA	Valvoline Oil Co., Division of Ashland Oil Inc., Ashland, Ky. 41114	Wht/Blu/Red	CP	80's	$3
1125	Valvoline Four Guard SAE 10W-30	Valvoline Oil Co., Ashland, Ky. 41114	Blu/Gld/Red/Wht	CP	80's	$4
1126	Valvoline Non Detergent	Valvoline Oil Co., Division of Ashland Oil, Ashland, Ky. 41101	Wht/Blu/Red	CP	80's	$3
1127	Valvoline Racing	Valvoline Oil Co., Division of Ashland Oil, Ashland, Ky. 41114	Wht/Blu/Red/Sil	CP	80's	$8
1128	Valvoline Racing 20W-50	Valvoline Oil Co., Division of Ashland Oil, Ashland, Ky. 41114	Wht/Blu/Red/Sil	CP	80's	$8
1129	Valvoline Super HPO	Valvoline Oil Co., Division of Ashland Oil, Ashland, Ky. 41114	Wht/Blu/Red/Cop	CP	80's	$4
1130	Valvoline Super HPO HD SAE 30	Valvoline Oil Co., Division of Ashland Oil, Ashland, Ky. 41114	Wht/Blu/Red	CP	80's	$4
1131	Valvoline Turbo V 10W-30	Valvoline Oil Co., Division of Ashland Oil, Ashland, Ky. 41101	Sil/Blu/Red	CP	80's	$4
1132	Valvoline Turbo V 20w-50	Valvoline Oil Co., Division of Ashland Oil, Ashland, Ky. 41101	Sil/Blu/Red	CP	80's	$4
1133	Valvoline Turbo V 20w-50	same as #-- except experimental white plastic lid	Sil/Blu/Red	CP	80's	$25
1134	Valvoline E-S-P	Valvoline Oil Co., Division of Ashland Oil Inc., Ashland, Ky. 41101	Sil/Blu/Red	CP	80's	$4
1135	Victory	Barnsdall Refining Corp., Tulsa, Ok.	Blu/Wht	SS	30's	$200
1136	Vitalized Heavy Duty	Montgomery Ward	Cop/Wht/Blu	SS	60's	$12
1137	Wards All Season	Montgomery Ward	Gry/Wht/Red	SS	50's	$60
1138	Wards Ice Guard	Montgomery Ward USA	Wht/Blu/Red	SS	30's	$100
1139	Wards Permanent Anti-freeze	Montgomery Ward, Chicago, Il.	Red/Wht	SS	40's	$45
1140	Wards 100% Pure Pennsylvania	Distributed by Montgomery Ward & Co. USA	Red/Blu/Wht	SS	40's	$35
1141	Wards 100% Pure Pennsylvania	Montgomery Ward USA	Red/Blk/Wht	SS	30's	$35
1142	Wards Vitalized Heavy Duty	Montgomery Ward	Blu/Wht	SS	50's	$40
1143	Wards Vitalized Premium Grade	Montgomery Ward	Mar/Wht	SS	40's	$25
1144	Waverly High Speed (w/PGCOA logo)	Waverly Oil Works Co., Pittsburgh U.S.A.	Wht/Blu/Red	SS	30's	$65
1145	Waverly High Speed "Permit No.11"	Waverly Oil Works Co., Pittsburgh U.S.A.	Wht/Blu/Red	SS	40's	$65
1146	Waverly High Speed Special Outboard	Waverly Oil Works Co., Pittsburgh U.S.A.	Wht/Blu/Red	SS	30's	$80
1147	Waverly Premium Grade	Waverly Petroleum Prod. Co., Philadelphia, Pa.	Wht/Blu/Red	SS	40's	$45
1148	WOW (Waverly Oil Works)	The Waverly Oil Works Co., Pittsburgh, Pa.	Crm/Blu/Red	SS	50's	$35

ALL PRICES LISTED IN THIS BOOK ARE FOR GRADE 9 CANS

1121-1134	Valvoline: See also 107 Beaver Penn, 337 Fort Pitt, 339-341 Freedom, 350-352 Galena, 1054 Tip Top Penn, 1100-1120 Valvoline
1135	Victory: See also 103, 104 Barnsdall, 105, 106 B Square, 645, 646 Monamotor, 974 Superoil
1136-1143	Vitalized - Wards: See also 648, 649 Montgomery Ward

 ☐ 1121
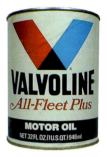 ☐ 1122
 ☐ 1123
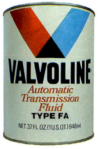 ☐ 1124
 ☐ 1125
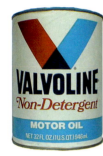 ☐ 1126
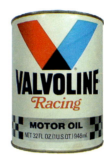 ☐ 1127

 ☐ 1128
 ☐ 1129
 ☐ 1130
 ☐ 1131
 ☐ 1132
 ☐ 1133
 ☐ 1134

 ☐ 1135
 ☐ 1136
 ☐ 1137
 ☐ 1138
 ☐ 1139
 ☐ 1140
 ☐ 1141

 ☐ 1142
 ☐ 1143
 ☐5 1144
 ☐ 1145
 ☐ 1146
 ☐5 1147
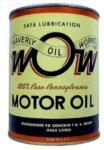 ☐ 1148

#	NAME	COMPANY	COLORS	MAT.	ERA	VALUE
1149	Weather Mate All Season Heavy Duty	Petroleum Chemicals Co., Danville, Ill/Los Angeles, Ca.	Yel/Brn/Wht/Blu	SS	50's	$75
1150	Western Mark 5 Heavy Duty	Western Oil and Fuel Co., Minneapolis, Mn.	Blu/Blu/Red/Wht	SS	50's	$60
1151	Western Mark 7 Extra Duty	Western Oil and Fuel Co., Minneapolis, Mn.	Gld/Wht/Blk/Ora	SS	50's	$60
1152	Western Reconditioned-Reclaimed	Western Oil Co. USA	Wht/Blu/Red	SS	50's	$125
1153	Western Reconditioned-Reclaimed	Western Oil Co. USA	Sil/Red	SS	70's	$75
1154	Wide World	(no company or location listed)	Wht/Red/Blu	SS	50's	$250
1155	Wil-Flo	Midwest Oil Co., Minneapolis, Fargo, Sioux Falls	Wht/Blu/Red	SS	40's	$250
1156	Wolf's Head	Wolf's Head Oil Refining Co., Oil City, Pa., New York, N.Y.	Sil/Grn/Red	SS	60's	$15
1157	Wolf's Head	Wolf's Head Oil Refining Co., Oil City, Pa., New York, N.Y.	Sil/Grn/Red	RS	60's	$30
1158	Wolf's Head ATF	Wolf's Head Oil Refining Co., Oil City, Pa.	Sil/Red/Grn	SS	60's	$20
1159	Wolf's Head Motor Oil	Wolf's Head Oil Refining Co., Oil City, Pa. 16301	Grn/Wht/Red	CP	70's	$5
1160	Wolf's Head Heavy Duty	Wolf's Head Oil Refining Co., Oil City, Pa. 16301	Wht/Grn/Red	CP	70's	$5
1161	Wolf's Head Multi-Duty	Wolf's Head Oil Refining Co., Oil City, Pa. 16301	Gld/Wht/Blk/Red	CP	80's	$5
1162	Wolf's Head Motor Oil Premium	Wolf's Head Oil Refining Co., Oil City, Pa. 16301	Grn/Wht/Red	CP	60's	$5
1163	Wolf's Head Racing	Wolf's Head Oil Refining Co., Oil City, Pa. 16301	Red/Wht/Blk	CP	80's	$12
1164	Wolf's Head Special Duty	Wolf's Head Oil Refining Co., Oil City, Pa. 16301	Blk/Wht/Red	CP	80's	$5
1165	Wolf's Head Super Duty	Wolf's Head Oil Refining Co., Oil City, Pa. 16301	Wht/Blk/Gld/Red	CP	70's	$5
1166	Work Force Non-Detergent	Work Force, Houston, Tx. 77242-2808	Blk/Ora/Yel/Chr	CP	80's	$8
1167	Zenoil	Zenith Oil Co., Butler, Pa.	Yel/Blu/Red/Wht	SS	30's	$75
1168	Zephyr	J.D. Street and Co. Inc., St Louis, Mo.	Red/Blu/Wht	SS	50's	$50
1169	Zephyr Premium	J.D. Street and Co. Inc., St Louis, Mo.	Blu/Red/Wht	SS	50's	$50
1170	Zephyr ATF Suffix A	J.D. Street and Co. Inc., St. Louis, Mo.	Wht/Red/Blu	SS	60's	$60
1171	Zephyr Super Heavy Duty	J.D. Street and Co. Inc.	Gld/Red/Blu/Wht	SS	60's	$40
1172	Zephyr LMO	J.D. Street and Co. Inc., St. Louis, Mo. 63110	Blu/Red/Gld/Wht	CP	80's	$12
1173	Zephyr Super LMO	J.D. Street and Co. Inc., St. Louis, Mo. 63110	Blu/Red/Gld/Wht	CP	80's	$12
1174	Zephyr LMO (no text in Zephyr Logo)	J.D. Street and Co. Inc., Maryland Heights, Mo. 63043	Blu/Gld/Wht/Red	CP	80's	$10
1175	Zoildeez	Pennzoil-South Penn Oil Co., Oil City, Pa.	Yel/Blk	SS	60's	$25
1176	Zoilube	Pennzoil Co.	Yel/Blk/Red	SS	30's	$65

ALL PRICES LISTED IN THIS BOOK ARE FOR GRADE 9 CANS

1149 Weather-Mate: See also 100 Armor, 101 Artic Flo, 115 Blue Star Anti-freeze, 838, 839 Protecto
1150, 1151 Western Mark 5, Western Mark 7: See also 588 Mileage
1155 Wil-Flo: See also 3-9 Ace, 584-587 Midwest, 643 MOCO
1156-1165 Wolf's Head: See also 236, 237 Empire
1168-1174 Zephyr: See also 404 HPX, 694 Penndurol
1175, 1176 Zoildeez, Zoilube: See also 415 Hydra-Flo, 682 Par-O-Vis, 683 Super Par-O-Vis, 708-750 Pennzoil, 1055, 1056 Tranzport

 1149
 1150
 1151
 1152
 1153
 1154
 1155
 1156
 1157
 1158
 1159
 1160
 1161
 1162
 1163
 1164
 1165
 1166
 1167
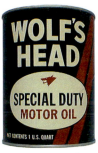 1168
 1169
 1170
 1171
 1172
 1173
 1174
 1175
 1176

Pennsylvania Grade Crude Oil Association Members
Information compiled as of January, 2003

This list was compiled from documenting cans in various collections along with a copy of the membership list of the Pennsylvania Grade Crude Oil Association from 1951. Although this list is extensive, it isn't complete. Any new information on P.G.C.O.A. numbers not listed here will be published in future volumes. If you have information on companies not listed below, please contact the authors. Any additions would be greatly appreciated.

Some numbers are listed twice with two different companies. It is believed that when a company dropped membership in the P.G.C.O.A., it's membership number was then assigned to another company. When a brand of oil changed ownership from one company to another, the P.G.C.O.A. number also transferred to the new company. An example of this is P.G.C.O.A. number 51 which originally was assigned to the Enterprise Oil company for the brand name "Duplex". When Quaker State purchased Enterprise, the P.G.C.O.A. membership number for Enterprise was assigned to Quaker State.

This list can be helpful in identifying the producer of a brand of oil that lists no company but does list the P.G.C.O.A. membership number such as can #705 Pennsyline. The can has no producer listed but the P.G.C.O.A. number identifies this brand as being marketed by the Bodie-Hoover Petroleum Corporation of Chicago.

0001	Sterling Oil Co., Oil City, Pa. (later Quaker State Oil Ref. Co.)	Sterling
0002	Pennzoil Oil Co., Oil City, Pa.	Pennzoil
0003	Kendall Refining Co., Bradford, Pa.	Kendall Penzbest
0004	Hyvis Oils Inc., Warren, Pa.	Hy Vis
0005	Oil Creek Refining Co., Titusville, Pa.	Oil Creek
0006	Wolf's Head Oil Refining Co., Inc., N.Y., N.Y.	Wolf's Head
0007	Continental Refining Co., Oil City, Pa.	Coreco
0008	Superior Oil Works, Warren, Pa.	Penn Eaton
0009	Canfield Oil Co., Cleveland, Oh.	Wm. Penn
0010	Bradford Oil Refining Co., Bradford, Pa.	All Penn
0011	Waverly Oil Works, Pittsburgh, Pa.	WOW
0012	Amalie Division/L. Sonneborn Sons Inc., N.Y., N.Y.	Amalie
0013	Ultra Penn Refining Co., Butler, Pa.	Ultra Penn
0014		
0015	Pennsylvania Refining Co., Butler, Pa.	PennDrake
0015	Dakota Independent Oil Co., Lemmon, S.D.	High Grade
0016	Pennsylvania Refining Co., Butler, Pa.	
0017	Tidewater Oil Co., New York	Veedol
0018		
0019	Wolf's Head Oil and Refining Co., N.Y., N.Y.	Wolf's Head
0020		

0021		
0022	Freedom-Valvoline Oil Co., Freedom, Pa.	Valvoline
0023		
0024	United Refining Co., Warren, Pa.	Emblem
0025	Elk Refining Co., Charleston, W.Va.	Elk
0026		
0027		
0028		
0029	Canfield Oil Co., Cleveland, Oh.	Wm Penn
0030	Franklin Refinery, A Div. of L. Sonneborn Sons, Inc., Franklin, Pa,	Sono Penn
0031	Freedom-Valvoline Oil Co., Freedom, Pa.	Freedom Perfect
0032	United Refining Co., Warren, Pa.	Emblem Powerlube
0033		
0034		
0035	Continental Refining Co., Oil City, Pa.	Coreco
0036	Pennsylvania Oil Products Refining Co., Warren, Pa.	
0036	Colorado and Utah Petroleum Co., Denver, Co.	Eldred
0037	The Pure oil Co., Chicago, Ill.	Tiolene
0038		
0039	National Refining Co., Cleveland, Oh.	En-Ar-Co
0040	Conewango Refining Co., Warren, Pa.	HY-VIS
0041	Tide Water Associated Oil Co., New York, N.Y.	TY Penn
0042		
0043		
0044		
0045	Calumet Refining Co., Chicago, Il., Cleveland, Oh.	Cal-Penn
0046		
0047	Richfield Oil Corp. of New York	Richlube
0048		
0049	W.H. Barber, Minneapolis, Mn.	Penno
0050	Quaker State Oil Refining Corp., Oil City, Pa.	Quaker State
0051	Enterprise Oil Co., Buffalo, N.Y.	Duplex Outboard
0051	Quaker State Oil Refining Corp., Oil City, Pa.	
0052		
0053		
0054	Christenson Oil Co., Portland, Or.	Real Penn
0055		
0056	Ultra Penn Refining Co., Butler, Pa.	Hard Wear Penn
0057	Venango Refining Co. Inc., Franklin, Pa.	Penn Born

0057	Franklin Ref., Div. of L Sonneborn Sons, Inc.	
0058		
0059	United Refining Co., Warren, Pa.	Seneca
0060	California Oil Co., Barber, N.J. (also New York, N.Y.)	Monogram
0061	Daugherty Refinery, Div. of L. Sonneborn Sons, Inc., New York, N.Y.	Penn Senior
0062	Wolf's Head Oil Refining Co. Inc.,	Penn Empire
0063		
0064	Tiona Petroleum Co., Philadelphia, Pa.	Tiopet
0065	Barnsdall Refining Corp.	Barnsdall Pennsylvania
0066		
0067	U.S. Oil Co., Providence, R.I.	U.S. Motor Oil
0068		
0069	West Penn Oil Co., Warren, Pa.	Oneida
0070		
0071	Pennsylvania Refining Co., Butler, Pa.	Cruiser
0072	Warren Refining Co., Warren, Pa.	Infallible
0072	Pierre A Brusselairs, Antwerp, Belgium	Penn Trump
0073	Famous Lubricants Inc., Chicago, Ill.	Motor Life Penn
0074	Franklin Refinery, A Div. of L. Sonneborn Sons Inc., Franklin, Pa.	Penn Milford
0075		
0076		
0077	Freedom Oil Co., Freedom, Pa.	Fort Pitt
0078	United Refining Co., Warren, Pa.	Lucky Penn
0079	Continental Refining Co., Oil City, Pa.	Continental Oil
0080	Magie Brothers, Chicago, Ill.	Rock-Penn
0081	Daugherty Refinery, A Div. of L. Sonneborn Sons Inc., New York, N.Y.	Penn Triumph
0082		
0083	Nott-Atwater Co., Spokane, Wn.	Naco
0084	Smith Oil and Refining Co., Rockford, Ill.	Super Penn
0085		
0086	Northland Products Co., Waterloo, Ia.	Northland
0087		
0088	Bartles-Shepard Oil Co., Waterloo, Ia.	
0088	Northland Products Co., Waterloo, Ia.	Northland
0089	Freedom Oil Works, Co., Freedom, Pa.	Penn Ace, Penn Trump
0090	Interstate Oil Co., Kansas City, Ks.	X-L Penn
0091		
0092	C. F. Battenfeld Oil Co., Detroit, Mich.	Bat-O-Co
0093	Lidsay-McMillan Co., Milwaukee, Wis.	Delcopenn

0094	Alliance Oil Co., Inc., New York, N.Y.	Alliance
0095	Allegheny-Arrow Oil Co., Canton, Oh.	Arrow
0096	Fiske Brothers Refining Co., Newark, N.J.	Lubroline
0097	Alemite Corp., Chicago, Il.	Alemite
0098	Franklin Refinery, Div. of L. Sonneborn Sons, Inc., Franklin, Pa.	Tri-More-Penn
0099	Wadhams Oil Co., Milwaukee, Wis	
0100		
0101		
0102	Tri-State Distributors Inc., Philadelphia, Pa.	Penn Tri-State
0103	Freedom Oil Co., Freedom, Pa.	Beaver-Penn
0104	Sovereign Oil Co., Chicago, Il.	
0105	Tiona Petroleum Co., Philadelphia, Pa.	V-800
0106	United Oil Co., Pittsburgh, Pa.	United
0107		
0108	American Oil Corp., Franklin, Pa.	Pennwize
0108	The Neville Co., Pittsburgh, Pa.	Pennpayz
0109	Tide Water Associated Oil Co., New York, N.Y.	Penn X-L-Ent
0110	Bradford Oil Distributing Co., Bradford, Pa.	All Pen
0111	New York Lubricating Oil Co., New York, N.Y.	Monogram
0112	United Petroleum Corp., Omaha	Uni-Penn
0112	Pennsylvania Petroleum Co., N. K.C. Mo.	Penncoil
0113		
0114		
0115	Superior Oil Works, Warren, Pa.	Pennsylvania
0116		
0117		
0118	E.F. Houghton & Co., Philadelphia, Pa.	Vital Deluxe
0119	Stevenson Oil and Chemical Co., Cleveland, Oh.	Peerless
0120	Penn-Crest Oil and Grease Corp., Long Island City, N.Y.	Penn-Crest
0121	Union Label Oil Co., Inc., New York, N.Y.	Unoil
0122	Ultra Penn Refining Co., Butler, Pa.	Prime Penn
0123	Canfield Oil Co., Cleveland, Oh.	Pennsylvania Premium
0124	Grand Penn Oil Co., Butler, Pa.	Grand Penn
0124	Pennsylvania Ref. Co.	
0125	Franklin Refinery, Div. of L. Sonneborn Sons, Inc., Franklin, Pa.	Unolene
0126	New York Lubricating Oil Co., New York, N.Y.	Excelsol
0127	The Powerine Co., Denver, Co.	Power-Lube
0128	Bodie-Hoover Petroleum Corp., Chicago, Ill.	Pennsyline
0129	Elk Refining Co., Charleston, W.Va.	Penn Patrol

0130		
0131	Bodie-Hoover Petroleum Corp., Lemont, Il. (later Chicago)	Pennstate
0132	Hudson Oil Co., Kansas City, Ks.	Pennvein
0133	Coronet Lubricants Co., Los Angeles, Ca.	Coronet
0134		
0135	Journal Oil Co., Bradford, Pa.	"B" Motor Oil
0136	Southern Oil Service, Inc., Nashville, Tn.	Apex
0137		
0138	Pennsylvania Refining Co., Butler, Pa.	P R X
0139	Western Auto Supply Co.	Super Good Penn
0140		
0141	Franklin Refinery, Div. of L Sonneborn Sons, Inc., Franklin, Pa.	Fred Meyer Penn
0142	Eagle Oil and Supply Co., Boston, Mass.	Eagleine (oil bottle)
0142	West Point Oil Co., Los Angeles, Ca.	Penn Rule
0143		
0144	Schaeffer Mfg. Co., St. Louis, Mo.	Security
0145		
0146		
0147		
0148	Harry B. Kitchin, Richmond, In.	Penn Wave
0149		
0150	Franklin Refinery, A Div. of L. Sonneborn Sons Inc., Franklin, Pa.	Penn Sylvan Airflight
0151	Pennsylvania Oil Products Refining Company	Penn National
0152		
0153		
0154		
0155	National Gas and Oil Co., Chicago, Ill.	Dutch State
0156	The Quaker Petroleum Co.	Pennfield
0156	Paraland Oil Co., Omaha, Neb.	Pennfield
0157	Spur Distributing Co., Nashville, Tn.	Golden Spur
0158	Apex Oil Products, Minneapolis Mn.	Penntrol
0159		
0160		
0161	The Ohio Oil Co., Findlay, Oh.	Marathon Penn
0162		
0163	Derby Oil Co., Wichita, Ks.	Penn Star
0164		
0165		
0166	Bradford Oil Refining Co., Bradford, Pa.	K-24

0167		
0168		
0169	Long Oil Co., Manhattan, Ks.	
0170		
0171	Canadian Petroleum Co. Ltd., Montreal, Quebec, Canada	Hot-Penn
0172		
0173		
0174		
0175	The Independent Lubricating Co., Topeka, Ks.	Penzene
0176	The Waverly Oil Works, Pittsburgh, Pa.	Mecca
0177	Gebhart Stores Inc.	Gebharts Gold Comet
0178		
0179		
0180		
0181	Bison Oil Products Co., Inc., Buffalo, N.Y.	Bisonoil
0182		
0183	Geo. C. Peterson Co., Chicago, Ill.	Pioneer
0184	Farmers Union Co-Operative Assoc., Wahoo, Neb.	Farmers Union Penn
0185	Pittsburgh Penn Oil Co., Pittsburgh, Pa.	Prize Penn
0185	Franklin Oil Co.	
0186	Idaho Ref. Co., Wasatch Oil Ref. Co., Inland Empire Ref. Inc.	Indian Penn
0187		
0188		
0189		
0190		
0191	C.F. Kellom and Co. Inc., Philadelphia, Pa.	Invader
0192		
0193		
0194	Sovereign Oil Co., Chicago, Ill.	Sovereign Dual Mileage
0195	Autolene Lubricants Co., Denver, Co.	Penn-O-Lene
0196		
0197		
0198		
0199		
0200	Douglas Oil Co. of Cal., Paramount, Ca.	Douglas
0201		
0202		
0203	Consumers Oil Co., Pawtuckett, RI.	Penn-State
0204	Alliance Oil Co., Inc., New York, N.Y.	Deluxe-Penn

0205	Allied Petroleum Corp., Chicago, Ill.	Pennlube
0206	Elk Refining Co., Charleston, W.Va.	Gold Flo
0207		
0208	Pioneer Oil Co., Philadelphia, Pa.	Safety-Lube
0209		
0210		
0211	Bell Oil Corporation, New York, N.Y.	Penn Craig
0212	Lake Shore Oil Co., Chicago, Ill.,	Crystal
0212	Crystal Motor Oil Company	
0213	W.B. Dick and Co. Inc., New York, N.Y.	Ilo-Penn
0214	Canfield Oil Co., Cleveland, Oh.	Dependable Penn
0215	Jobbers Oil Products Co., Oshkosh, Wis.	Oil-Rite
0216		
0217		
0218	Midwest Oil Co., Minneapolis, Fargo, Sioux Falls	Ace High
0219		
0220	Pontiac Oil Co. Ltd., Montreal, Quebec, Canada	Hero-Penn
0221		
0222		
0223	Aktiebolaget Axel Christiernsson, Stockholm, Sweden	Pennax
0224	Western Auto Supply Co., Kansas City, Mo.	Good Penn
0225		
0226	Clover Farm Stores Corp., Cleveland, Oh.	Clover Penn
0227		
0228	Kern Oil Co. Ltd., Los Angeles, Ca.	Kern Penn
0229		
0230		
0231	U.S. Oil Co., Providence, R.I.	Penn-Velvet
0232	Gilmore Oil Co., Los Angeles, Ca.	Lion Head Pennsylvania
0233		
0234		
0235		
0236	The Goyer Co., Greenville, Miss.	Pure Gold
0237		
0238		
0239		
0240		
0241	Columbia-Bedford Corp., New York, N.Y.	Penn-More
0242		

0243	San Francisco Garage Owners Assoc., Ltd., San Francisco, Ca.	Acme Penn
0244		
0245		
0246	Franklin Oil & Gas Co., Bedford, Oh.	Duroil Pennsylvania
0247		
0248		
0249		
0250		
0251	Hancock Oil Co.	
0252		
0253		
0254	Lou-Bob Co., Chicago, Il.	Lou-Bob Pennsylvania
0255		
0256	Union Trading Co. Inc., New York, N.Y.	Pennalux
0257	Fletcher Oil Co., Boise, Id.	Veltex Penn
0258	Pennsylvania Oil Co., Somerville, Mass.	Penn-Protector
0259		
0260	The Cincinnati Vulcan Co., Inc., Cincinnati, Oh.	Vulcan
0261	The Star Oil Co., Chicago, Ill.	Gold Star
0262	Imperial Oil Ltd., Toronto, Ontario, Canada	Royal-Penn
0263		
0264	Victory Oil Co., Inc., Arabi, La.	Vic-Penn
0265		
0266		
0267	Biron Oil Co., Chicago, Ill.	Bironoil
0268	Iowa Farm Service Co., Des Moines, Ia.	IOA-Penn
0269		
0270	Pennsylvania Refining Co., Butler, Pa.	Dean Penn
0271		
0272	Colorado Petroleum Products Co., Denver, Co.	Precision
0273		
0274	Fox River Valley Co-op, Appleton, Wi.	Fox Cooperative
0275		
0276	H.K. Stahl Co., St. Paul, Minn.	Crown Penn
0277	H.F. Harold, Northwood, England	Harold Penn
0278		
0279	Penola Oil Co., New York, N.Y.	Penotol
0280		
0281		

0282		
0283		
0284	Signal Oil Co., Los Angeles, Ca.	Signal Penn
0285	Illinois Oil Co., Rock Island, Ill.	Illoco-Penn, Welch-Penn
0286		
0287		
0288	The R.J. Brown Co., St. Louis, Mo.	Multi-Miles
0289		
0290	Mich-I-Penn Oil and Grease Co., Detroit, Mich.	Super Penn
0291	Penn Glenn Oil Works Inc., Leechburg, Pa.	Glen-Lube
0292	Ray Brothers Oil Co., Long Beach, Ca.	Tru Vis
0293		
0294		
0295		
0296		
0297		
0298		
0299		
0300	Southern Oil Co. of New York Inc., Horseheads, N.Y.	Rotary
0301	Columbia Oil Co., Inc., St. Louis, Mo.	Pensy
0302		
0303		
0304		
0305		
0306		
0307		
0308	The Pennzoil Co., Oil City, Pa.	Tough Film
0309	L.D. Ohm Co., Moose Jaw, Saskatchewan, Canada	Pedigree Penn
0310	Fisher Foods, Cleveland, Oh.	Can-O-Gold
0311		
0312		
0313		
0314		
0315		
0316	Gambles Stores, Minneapolis, Mn. (later Gambles-Skogmo)	Gamble's
0317		
0318	Southern Oil Service, Inc., Nashville, Tenn.	Penn-Gold
0319		
0320	Riley Brothers Inc., Burlington, Ia.	R.B. 500

0321	Modern Petroleum Corp., Philadelphia, Pa.	State Seal Pennsylvania
0322	Dacus Oil Co., San Francisco, Ca.	Ring Seal Penn
0323		
0324	Shamrock Oil and Gas Corp., Amarillo, Tx.	Shamrock Penn
0325	Famous Department Stores Inc., Los Angeles, Ca.	Penn Pilot
0326		
0327		
0328		
0329		
0330	William Roth and Sons Oil Co. of New York Westbury	Penn Rolene
0331	Westmoreland Oil and Gas Co., Greensburg, Pa.	Wesco
0332	Parmelee Motor Fuel Co., Pittsburgh, Pa.	Parmoco
0333		
0334		
0335	Black Bear Co., Inc., Long Island City, N.Y.	Black Bear
0336	Fair Price Petroleum Co., Yankton, S.D.	Gurney
0337		
0338	South Side Petroleum Co., Chicago, Ill.	Dutch Mill
0339		
0340		
0341	Schock Independent Oil Co., Mount Joy, Pa.	Penn Joy
0342		
0343		
0344		
0345	Graham-Penn Oil Co., Houston, Tx.	Graham Pennsylvania
0346		
0347	Economy Boys Stores	Black Gold
0348	National Petroleum Co., New York, N.Y.	Napco Penn
0349	United Co-Operatives Inc., Indianapolis, In.	Bureau Penn
0350		
0351		
0352	Paxtang Oil Co., Paxtang, Harrisburg, Pa.	Fil-Lube
0353		
0354	Shellhorn and Hill Inc., Wilmington, Del.	Delolene
0355		
0356		
0357		
0358	Pennsylvania Refining Co., Butler, Pa.	Penn Banner
0359		

0360	Jewel Lubricants Inc., Chicago, Ill.	Jewel Penn
0361		
0362		
0363	Wright Oil Co., San Antonio, Tx.	Penn-Wright
0364	Maritime Petroleum Corp., New York, N.Y.	Flying Cloud
0365	Cadillac Oil Co., Detroit, Mich	Pennoline
0366	Mohawk Petroleum Co., San Francisco, Ca.	Mohawk Pennsylvania
0367		
0368	Vacuum Oil Co. Pty. Ltd., Melbourne, (Victoria), Australia	Progress Penn
0369		
0370		
0371		
0372	Champlain Oil Products Ltd.	Penmark
0373	Clark's Super Gas Co., Milwaukee, Wis.	Clark's Super Penn
0373	Crystal Motor Oil Co., Chicago, Ill.	
0374	Societe Commerciale des Produits, Paris, France	Luxtra
0375	Royal 400 Oil Co., Fort Dodge, Ia.	Loyal Penn
0376	Wm. Penn Gas Co., Inc., Lyons, Ill.	Power Penn
0377		
0378	Transco Oil Co., Los Angeles, Ca.	Pennian
0379	The Hancock Oil Co., of California, Long Beach, Ca.	Hancock Pennsylvania
0380	Wolf's Head Oil Refining Co., Inc., Oil City, Pa.	Venango
0381		
0382		
0383		
0384		
0385		
0386		
0387	B. F. Goodrich Co., Akron, Oh./Los Angeles, Ca	Penrich
0388		
0389	Western Oil and Fuel Co., Minneapolis, Minn.	Husky
0390	Hochelaga Petroleum Co., Montreal, Quebec, Canada	Penn-Norac
0391		
0392	Quaker State Oil Refining Corp., Oil City, Pa.	Oilvania
0393		
0394	Johnson Oil Refining Co., Chicago, Il.	Brilliant Penn
0395		
0396	Banner Mfg. Co. Inc., Brooklyn, N.Y.	Penn-Signet
0397		

0398		
0399	Monoplane Oil Co., Div. of Lasky Bros., Inc., Newark, N.J.	Aerolube
0400		
0401	Pennsylvania Refining Co., Butler, Pa.	Yankee
0402		
0403		
0404		
0405	Quaker City Oil Co., Bradford, Pa.	
0406		
0407	Custer City Oil Co., Bradford, Pa.	Preferred Penn
0408	Mich-I-Penn Oil and Grease Co., Detroit, Mich.	Oak Penn
0409		
0410		
0411		
0412	R.A. Hyde Oil Co., Pipestone, Minn.	Hyde's Pride
0413		
0414		
0415		
0416	Lou-Bob Co., Chicago, Ill.	Superlene
0417	National Dixie Distributors, Inc., Ann Arbor, Mich.	Dixie Penn
0418		
0419		
0420		
0421	Heim and Lundin A/S, Oslo, Norway	Pennalub
0422	Century Oil Co., Long Beach, Ca.	Century
0423		
0424		
0425	Sterns Ltd., London, England	Solexol
0426	Supreme Petroleum Products Co., Inc., Philadelphia, Pa.	Prime-Lube
0427	Our Own Hardware Co., Minneapolis, Minn.	Our Own Pure Penn
0428	H.K. Stahl Co.	Admiral Penn
0429		
0430	Tide Water Associated Oil Co., New York, N.Y.	Super Body
0431		
0432		
0433		
0434	Wisconsin Cooperative Farm Supply Co., Madison, Wis.	Farmco Penn
0435		
0436	Apex Oil and Lubricants Co., Brooklyn, N.Y.	Durabilt

0437		
0438	Hindusthan Oil Distributing Co., Calcutta, India	Penn-Star
0439		
0440		
0441		
0442		
0443		
0444		
0445	Aktiebolaget Axel Christiernsson, Stockholm, Sweden	Indian Pennsylvania
0446	Seaside Oil Co., Santa Barbara, Ca.	Seaside Pennsylvania
0447	Majestic Lubricating Co., Tulsa, Ok.	Penna-jestic
0448		
0449		
0450	Oklahoma Tire and Supply Co., Oklahoma City, Ok.	Penn Otasco
0451	Skandinavisk-Amerikanska Petroleum A/B, Stockholm, Sweden	Vast Penn
0452	H. C. Sleigh, Ltd., Melbourne, Australia	Golden Fleece Penn
0453		
0454	Sweney Gasoline and Oil Co., Peoria, Ill.	Gold Penn
0455	Curry Oil Co., Boston, Mass.	Superba
0456	Direct Service Oil Co., Minneapolis, Mn.	Super Servis
0457	A.W. Harris Oil Co., Providence, RI.	Harris
0458	Arrow Oil Co., Baltimore, Md.	Penn Arrow
0459		
0460	Shoobsol Co., Passaic, N.J.	Super Lafayette
0461	Time Oil Co., Los Angeles, Ca.	Time Penn
0462		
0463		
0464		
0465		
0466		
0467	Penn Wealth Oils Pty. Ltd., Sydney, (N.S.W.), Australia	Penn Wealth
0468	Kern Oil Co., Ltd., Los Angeles, Ca.	St. Helens Penn
0469	Boler Petroleum Co., Philadelphia, Pa.	Bo-Penn
0470		
0471		
0472		
0473		
0474	Republic Oil Refining Co., N.Y./Pittsburgh/Houston	Rocolene
0474	Marathon Oil Co., Republic Division	

0475		
0476		
0477		
0478		
0479	Pennoak Oil Co., Ltd., Montreal, Quebec, Canada	Pennoak
0480	Laird Inc., Los Angeles, Ca.	Sta-Lube
0481	Calstate Refining Co., Long Beach, Ca.	Calstate Pennsylvania
0482	Keystone Lubricating Co., Philadelphia, Pa.	Keystone
0483	Petroleum Specialties, Inc., New York, N.Y.	Filtrapenn
0484		
0485		
0486	The Molyneaux Co., Philadelphia, Pa.	Stanalone
0487	High Penn Oil Co. Inc., High Point, N.C.	High Penn
0488		
0489		
0490		
0491	Southern States Oil Co., Jacksonville, Fl.	Southern States Pennsylvania
0492		
0493		
0494	Societe Commerciale des Produits, Paris, France	Lubrolux
0495	Diamond Gas and Fuel Co., Denver, Co.	Dixie Penn
0496		
0497		
0498	London Oil Co., London, Ontario, Canada	Penn-High
0499		
0500	Harbor Refining Co., Los Angeles, Ca.	Harbor Pennsylvania
0501		
0502		
0503	Farmers Gas and Oil Co. of Michigan, Ithica, Mich.	Fargo Penn
0504	Apex Motor Fuel Co., Chicago, Ill.	Radi-O-Lene
0505	Kocolene Co., Inc., Seymour, In.	Super Kocolene
0506		
0507		
0508		
0509	Roosevelt Oil Co., Mt Pleasant, Mi.	
0510	Nourse Oil Co., Kansas City, Mo.	Penn Power
0511		
0512	J&R Motor Supply Co.	J&R
0513		

0514		
0515		
0516	MFA Oil Co., Columbia, Mo.	Penn Guard
0517		
0518	Barnes Oil Co., Grand Rapids, Mich.	Town Talk Penn
0519	Mid-West Oil Co., Kansas City, Ks.	Penn Aero
0520	Marathon Lubricant Co., Fort Worth, Tx	Camel Penn
0521	Industrial Oil Corp., Warren, Pa.	Pennsylvania, Penn Hills
0522	Super-Penn Oil Co., Philadelphia, Pa.	Super-Penn
0523		
0524		
0525	William A. Evans, Buffalo, N.Y.	Iroquois
0526	Automotive Products Ltd., Carlton N.3, (Victoria), Australia	Penn (AP) Penn
0527	Viscosity Oil Co., Chicago, Il./Oil City, Pa.	Grai-Penn
0528	Consolidated Supply Co., Long Island City, N.Y.	Cosco
0529	Quincy Oil Co., Quincy, Mass.	Valora
0530		
0531		
0532		
0533	Guardian Oil Co., Port Newark, N.J.	
0534		
0535		
0536		
0537		
0538		
0539		
0540		
0541		
0542		
0543	Paragon Oil Co. Inc., Brooklyn, N.Y.	Paralene
0544	J.L. Quimby and Co., New York, N.Y.	Quim-Bee
0545		
0546	Paragon Oil Co. Inc., Brooklyn, N.Y.	Parapure
0547		
0548	The Deep Valley Oil Co., Barberton, Oh.	Positive Penn
0549	Washington Petroleum Products, Inc., Washington, D.C.	Lubeseal
0550		
0551	Maurice Jennings Pty. Ltd., Sydney, (N.S.W.), Australia	Penn Avon
0552		

0553		
0554	Sears Roebuck and Co., Chicago, Il.	Allstate, Cross Country
0555	Cato Oil and Grease Co., Oklahoma City, Ok.	Penntroleum
0556		
0557		
0558	Vacuum Oil Co., Pty. Ltd., Melbourne, (Victoria), Australia	
0559	Pennstate Lubricants Co., Chicago, Ill.	Dependon
0560		
0561		
0562		
0563	Sociedade Nacional de Petroleos, Lisbon, Portugal	Sonap
0564		
0565	Arthur C Withrow Co., Los Angeles, Ca.	Withrows Premium
0566		
0567	Jacques S. Nahama, Athens Greece	Big Penn
0568	Peters Oil Co., Chicago, Il.	Peter Penn, Gold Flo
0569		
0570	J.D. Street and Co. Inc., St Louis, Mo.	Penndurol, Zephyr
0571	Gaseteria, Inc., Indianapolis, In.	Phil-A-Penn
0572	Van Ness Oil Co., San Francisco, Ca.	Van Ness
0573	Skandinavisk-Amerikanska Petroleum A/B, Stockholm, Sweden	Sapenol
0574	company unknown	Penn-Lee
0575		
0576	Associated Petroleum Co. of Australia, Sydney (N.S.W.), Australia	Penn Will
0577	Arthur Vale & Co. Pty. Ltd., Port Melbourne, (Victoria), Australia	Valcol
0578		
0579		
0580		
0581		
0582	National Petroleum Ltd., Montreal, Quebec, Canada	Rapid Penn
0583		
0584		
0585		
0586		
0587	Warren Oil Co., Omaha, Neb.	Gold Bond
0588		
0589	Jean Osterwalder and Co., St. Gall Switzerland	Ostrol
0590	Reliance Oil Co., Flint, Mich.	Reliance Penn
0591	Union Supply Co., Pittsburgh, Pa.	USCO

0592	Denny Clepper, Wichita, Ks./Homer C. Jennings, Hutchinson, Ks.	HiPower Penn
0593	Keystone Oil Refining Co., Detroit, Mi. (also Victor Oil Co.)	Key-Penn
0594		
0595		
0596	W.C. Robinson and Son Co., Baltimore, Md.	Pennpure
0597	Perfect Power Corporation, Chicago, Ill.	Triple A-1 Penn
0598	company and location unknown	Star De-Penn-Flo
0599		
0600		
0601		
0602	Mich-I-Penn Oil and Grease Co., Detroit, Mich.	Penn Master
0603		
0604		
0605		
0606	Montgomery Ward and Co., Chicago, Ill.	Wards Supreme Quality
0607	Quality Oil Products Co., Milwaukee, Wis.	Quality Penn
0608	Sea Gull Lubricants Inc., Cleveland, Oh.	Sea Gull
0609		
0610		
0611	Milder Oil Co., Omaha, Neb.	Milderene
0612	Carpenter Oil Inc., Lincoln, Ne.	Supervania
0613	H.C. Sleigh Limited, Melbourne, Australia	Penn Summit
0614	Strauss Stores Corporation, Maspeth, N.Y.	Travelene
0615	Eduardo Osorio R., Puebla, Mexico	Penn Osoco
0616		
0617		
0618		
0619	Security Oil Co., Inc., Baltimore, Md.	Security Pennsylvania
0620	W.A. Wood Co., Boston, Mass.	Pennwood
0621		
0622		
0623	Dunlap, Mellor and Co., Philadelphia, Pa.	Dusco
0624	Northwestern Oil Co., Omaha, Neb.	EN-AR-CO Penn
0625	Star Service and Petroleum Co., Centralia, Ill.	Star Premium
0626	Industrial Oil Corp., Warren, Pa.	Penn Manor
0627		
0628	Oil Service Co., Warren, Pa.	Certol
0629	Petroleos Mexicanos, Mexico D.F., Mexico	Pemex Penn
0630	Illinois Farm Supply Co., Chicago, Il.	Penn Bond

0631	Frontier Refining Co., Denver, Co.	Frontier Penn
0632		
0633	Phoenix Oil Co., Augusta, Ga.	Safety Penn
0634		
0635	Penn-Field Oil Co., Chicago, Ill.	Golden State
0636		
0637		
0638	Jacques S. Nahama, Athens, Greece	Megapenn
0639	Farmers Union Central Exchange, Inc., St. Paul, Minn.	Penn Union
0640		
0641	Brais & Frere, Montreal, Quebec, Canada	Major-Penn
0642	Atlas Lubricant Corp., New Orleans La.	Atlas-Aero
0643	Viscosity Oil Co., Chicago, Ill.	Viscosity Penn
0644	United Petroleum Corp., Philadelphia, Pa.	Victor
0645	Emil Hauptmann & Volckmar, Hamburg, Germany	Penn-O-Lene
0646		
0647	Ohlcen and Nilsson Aktiebolag, Stockholm, Sweden	Globe Success Penn
0647	Pennsylvania Lub Oil Works, Rotterdam, Holland	
0648	Sunset Oil Co., Los Angeles, Ca.	Sunset Pennsylvania
0649	Beaurepaire Tyre Service Pty. Ltd., Melbourne, (Victoria), Australia	Penncyline
0650		
0651	Societe Commerciale des Produits, Paris, France	Pennextra
0652	Usol A.G., Basle, Switzerland	Loco Penn
0653	Australian Petroleum Co., Brisbane (Queensland), Australia	Maxim Penn
0654	John Pritzlaff Hardware Co., Milwaukee, Wis.	Everkeen
0655	J Maitzen Taifinoil u Speedoil, Vienna, Austria	Taifunoil
0656	Block Distributing Co., Yakima, Wn.	CQ Pennsylvania
0657	Barkow Petroleum Co., Richmond, Ca.	Diamond B
0658	Svenka AB Alfred Olsen and Co., Stockholm, Sweden	Philarine
0659		
0660	Australian Petroleum Co., Brisbane (Queensland) Australia	Major Penn
0661		
0662		
0663	L. M. Crane and Co., Boston, Mass.	Cranepenn
0664	Vargo Gas and Oil Co., Warren, Oh.	Buckeye State
0665	C.F. Mason Oil Co., Inc., Pittsburgh, Pa.	Penn-Mason
0666		
0667		
0668	Minnesota Farm Bureau Service Co., St. Paul, Mn.	Gopher Penn

0669		
0670	Sunset Oil Co., Los Angeles, Ca.	Sunset Penn
0671		
0672	Arrow Oil Co., Baltimore, Md.	Waller
0673		
0674		
0675		
0676	Mid-West Oil Co., Minneapolis, Fargo, Sioux Falls	Ace High
0677	The National Marketing Co., Oklahoma City, Ok.	EN-AR-CO Penn
0678	All American Petroleum, Co., Chicago, Ill.	Ampeco Penn
0679	Huileries Anversoises "Pierets", Antwerp, Belgium	Lubril Special
0680	Pruitt Petroleum Co., Philadelphia, Pa.	Pruitt 100% Pure Pennsylvania
0681	The Pennfield Oil Co., Omaha, Neb.	Pennfield
0682		
0683	Mercantil Martinez, S.A., Monterrey, N.L., Mexico	Gold Medal
0684	Consumers Co-Operative Associated, Amarillo, Tx	Penn CO-OP
0685	The Seedman Co., Inc., Brooklyn, N.Y.	Seedman Certified Gold Bond
0686	South Side Petroleum Co., Chicago, Ill.	Dixie Penn
0687	W.H. Barber Co., Chicago, Ill.	Pennada
0688	Mich-I-Penn Oil and Grease Co., Detroit, Mich.	Mid-west Service Pennsylvania
0689	Graham-Penn Oil Co., Houston, Tx.	Penn-Lac
0690		
0691	Farmers Union State Exchange, Omaha, Neb.	Statex Penn
0692		
0693	Heller Petroleum Corp., New York, N.Y.	Cahelco-Penn
0694	Longshore Petroleum Corp., New York, N.Y.	Penn Hills
0695	Litten Gas and Oil Service, East Liverpool, Ohio, Wheeling, W.Va.	Pennlit
0696		
0697	W.H. Barber Co., Chicago, Ill.	Fortified Penn
0698	Tiona Petroleum Co., Philadelphia, Pa.	Saicil Penn
0699		
0700	Mich-I-Penn Oil and Grease Co., Detroit, Mich.	Duro 100% Pure Pennsylvania
0701		
0702		
0703	Ryerson Oil Co., Inc., New York, N.Y.	Ryoco-Penn
0704	Etablissements Callot & De Schryver, S.A., Antwerp, Belgium	Avio
0705		
0706	Pennsylvania Petroleum Products Co., Philadelphia, Pa.	Quaker City
0707	Columbia-Bedford Corp., New York, N.Y.	Penn-Airliner

0707	Wright Oil Co., Jersey City, N.J.	
0708	Craig Oil Co., Inc., Oakland, Ca.	Craig Pennsylvania
0709		
0710	Pennsylvania Lub Oil Works, Rotterdam, Holland	Auto-Avia-Penn
0711		
0712	The United Oil Co. Inc., Baltimore, Md.	Duralene Pennsylvania
0713	A Lesire, G. Bruyndonckx & Co., Scheut-Brussels, Belgium	Elbe-Penn
0714	United States Oil Co., Rotterdam, Holland	Usol
0715		
0716		
0717		
0718	Guinn Oil Co., Chetopa, Ks.	Penn-Guinn
0719	Ryerson Oil Co., Inc., New York, N.Y.	Sacor
0720	Pennsylvania Petroleum Products Co., East Providence, R.I.	Penco
0721	Valley Oil Co., Salinas, Ca.	Valopenn
0722	American Refiners Outlet, Inc., Chicago, Ill.	Amro Penn
0723	Rock Oil Corp., Buffalo, N.Y.	Penn Rock
0724	Wynne Oil Co., Philadelphia, Pa.	Ronson
0725		
0726	Commerce Oil Corp., Warren, Pa.	Commerce 1000 Series
0727	National Solvent Corp., Cleveland, Oh.	Nasco Penn
0728		
0729		
0730	True's Oil Co., Spokane, Wn.	Rainbow Penn
0731	S.A. Sadonia, La Louviere, Belgium	Sadonia-Penn
0732	Christopher Oil Co., Prescott, Ark.	Penn-Cris
0733	Monarch Petroleum Products, Columbus, Oh.	Monarch Penn
0734	A.N. Karayusuf, Antakya, Turkey	Karayusuf Penn
0735	Pax Products Co., New York, N.Y.	Pennpax
0736	Graham-Penn Oil Co., Houston, Tx.	99 Penn
0737	Oel-Brack A.G., Aarau, Switzerland	Perfectol
0738	Dean Phipps Stores, Inc., Scranton, Pa.	Dyna-Penn
0739	Caminol Co., Hanford, Ca.	Beacon Pennsylvania
0740	Bowzer Oil Co., Macon, Mo.	Bowzer's Penn
0741	Charles Engels, Brussels, Belgium	Carterine Pennsylvania
0742	K Allan and Co., Ltd., Cheltenham, Gloucestershire, England	Alanzol Pennalub
0743		
0744	Cie Belgo-Americaine des Petroles, Ghent, Belgium	Black Eagle
0745	Usol A.G., Basle, Switzerland	Usol

0746	Haji Hussein Al Faiz, Ashar Basrah, Iraq	Lion of Babylon Penn
0747		
0748	United Petroleum Products S.A., Brussels, Belgium	Uppenn
0749	Pennland Lubricants Co., Philadelphia/Kansas City/Los Angeles	Pennland
0750	Modern Petroleum Corporation, Philadelphia, Pa.	Modern Pennsylvania
0751	The Travelon Oil Co., Rochester, N.Y.	Nysad-Penn
0752		
0753		
0754		
0755		
0756		
0757		
0758	Cussins & Fearn Co., Columbus, Oh.	Super Life
0759		
0760		
0761		
0762	Weber Oil Co., Inc., New York, N.Y.	Webco
0763		
0764		
0765	Northwestern Oil Co. of Nebraska, Omaha, Ne.	Northwestern Pennsylvania
0766		
0767		
0768		
0769		
0770		
0771		
0772		
0773		
0774		
0775		
0776		
0777	Vortex Petroleum, Co., Indianapolis, In. (later Hoosier Petr. Co., Inc.)	Vortex
0778	Hi-way Refineries Ltd.	Super Penn
0779		
0780	The Pennzoil Co., Oil City, Pa.	Coast 2 Coast
0781		
0782	The Delong Co., Clinton, Wis	Jay Dee
0783	Simonson Lumber and Supply Co., St Paul, Minn.	Cash Way Penn
0784	France Oil Co., Philadelphia, Pa.	Penngaloil Pennsylvania

0785		
0786	Miller & Holmes, Inc., St. Paul, Minn.	M&H Pennsylvania
0787	Niagara Lubricant Co. Inc., Buffalo, N.Y.	NiaPenn
0788	Industrial Oil Corp., Warren, Pa.	Penn-Wyn
0789	Tiona Petroleum Co., Philadelphia, Pa.	Arfield Pennsylvania
0790	National Lubricants Corp., Houston, Tx.	National Penn
0791		
0792	Lake Shore Oil Co., Chicago, Il	Ravenoyl
0793		
0794		
0795		
0796		
0797		
0798	Pennant Oil and Grease Co., L. A., Ca. (also Golden Bear Oil Co.)	Penn Franklin
0799		
0800		
0801	The Petroleum Lubricants Co. Inc., Baltimore, Md.	Penndura
0802		
0803		
0804	Mich-I-Penn Oil and Grease Co., Detroit, Mich.	Mich-I-Penn
0805		
0806	Pruitt Petroleum Co., Inc.,	Star Pennsylvania
0807		
0808		
0809	Delaware Oil Co. Ltd., London, England	Penextra
0810		
0811	S.A. des Usines Lauwers-Masurel, Brussels, Belgium	40 H Penn
0812		
0813	Commerce Oil Corp., Warren, Pa.	Comet 100% Pure Pennsylvania
0814		
0815	Etablissements Callot & De Schryver, S.A., Antwerp, Belgium	Penncen
0816	Marathon Oil and Grease Co., Mexico, D.F., Mexico	Haward Penn
0817	Crystal Motor Oil Co., Chicago, ill.	Colonial Penn
0818		
0819	United States Oil Co., Rotterdam, Holland	Unic
0820		
0821		
0822	Red Head Oil Co. (of Ohio), Brilliant, Oh.	Red Head
0823	Penola Oil Co., New York, N.Y.	Thor Penn

0824	Allied Wax and Oil Products Corp., New York, N.Y.	Arama
0825	E.H. Kellogg and Co., New York, N.Y.	Gorgon
0826	S.A. des Huikles Renault, Merksem, Belgium	Renault Penn Oil
0827	United States Oil Corp., New York, N.Y.	Penn-Index
0828	Clarkson and Ford Co., Clifton, N.J.	Banner 100% Penna
0828	Karl Sottiaux Fils, Antwerp, Belgium	Pennchief
0829	Georges Halff, Lausanne, Switzerland	Satol Penn
0830	Federal Oil Co., Los Angeles, Ca.	Federal Pennsylvania
0831		
0832		
0833		
0834	Erickson Brothers, Minneapolis, Minn.	Meroil Penn
0835	Huilerie "Macoil", Denderbelle, Belgium	Pennac
0836		
0837	The National Marketing Co., Oklahoma City, Ok.	NA-MAR-CO Penn
0838	Penn State Oil Co., Philadelphia, Pa.	Brytol Super Service
0839		
0840	United Petroleum Corporation, Portland, Or.	U.P.C. 100% Penn
0841		
0842	Red Diamond Oil Co. Inc., Pickens, S.C.	Diamolene
0843	Transmarine Oil Co., Inc., New York, N.Y.	Penarine
0844	Novera Inc., New York, N.Y.	Novera Pure Penn
0845		
0846		
0847	Cal Stores	Cal Pennsylvania
0847	Tennessee Valley Cooperatives, Inc., Decatur, Ala.	T.V. CO-OP
0848		
0849	Viscosity Oil Co., Chicago, Ill.	Viscosity Penn
0850	Viscosity Oil Co., Chicago, Ill.	Simmac Penn
0851		
0852	Delaware Oil Co. Ltd., London, England	Lubrolux
0853		
0854	Peoples Self-Service Gas Stations, Inc., Annandale, Va.	Peoples Motor Oil
0855	Schaefer & Carter, Brisbane, (Queensland), Australia	Penn Sylvan
0856	Schaeffer Bros. & Powell Manufacturing Co., St. Louis, Mo.	Evergreen
0857		
0858		
0859	The Beaver Oil Co. Ltd., Outremont, Montreal, Quebec, Canada	Monarch
0860	Northern Lubricating Co., Norwood, N.Y.	Norlube Pennsylvania

0861		
0862		
0863		
0864		
0865	company and location unknown	Evercool
0865	Riley Bros., Inc., Burlington, Ia.	Riley Bros. Pure Pennsylvania
0866	S.A. Sadonia, La Louviere, Belgium	Stratosoil
0867		
0868	Site Oil Co.	Five Star Penn
0868	Columbia Oil Co. Inc., St. Louis, Mo.	Five Star Penn
0869		
0870		
0871	Southern Petroleum Co., Inc., Memphis, Tn.	Southern's Pennsylvania Oil
0872		
0873	C.S. Young, East Orange, N.J.	Pencraft
0874		
0875		
0876	Republic Oil Refining Co., Pittsburgh, Pa.	Penn Sharp
0877		
0878		
0879	Smith-Allen Co., Los Angeles, Ca.	Industrial Penn
0880	Booster Motor Oil Co., Philadelphia, Pa.	Booster
0881	Hansen and Jenson Oil Co., Escanaba, Mich.	H & J Penn
0882		
0883		
0884		
0885	Bradford Gasoline Co., Bradford, Pa.	Brad-Penn
0886	The Crystal Flash Petroleum Corp., Indianapolis, Ind.	Penn Flash
0887		
0888		
0889		
0890		
0891		
0892	Sea Way Refining Co.	Sea Way
0893		
0894	Sterns Ltd., London, England	Re-Di-Penn
0895	C.R. Ware Oil Co., Springfield, Ill.	Wareco Penn
0896		
0897	Zenith Oil Co., Butler, Pa.	Zenoil

0897	Marshall-Wells Co., Duluth, Mn.	Zenoil
0898		
0899		
0900		
0901		
0902	Penn Glen Oil Works, Leechburg, Pa.	PG Pennsylvania Premium
0903		
0904		
0905	Morris and Co. (Shrewsbury) Limited, Shrewsbury (Shropshire), England	Golden Film Pennsylvania
0906		
0907		
0908	Karl Sottiaux Fils, Waret-La-Chaussee, Belgium	Road-Penn
0909		
0910		
0911		
0912		
0913	C. M. Clay's Sons, Poughkeepsie, N.Y.	Clay's Penn
0914	Staten Island Oil Co., Inc., Travis, Staten Island, N.Y.	Staten Island Oil Co. 100% Pure Pennsylvania Motor Oil
0915		
0916		
0917	Ambrose Company, South Norfolk, Va.	Fountain-Penn
0918		
0919	W.H. Barber Co., Chicago, Ill.	Penbar
0920		
0921		
0922	Pittsburgh Penn Oil Co., Pittsburgh, Pa.	Penn Leader
0923	Owl Oil and Supply Co., Union City, N.J.	Owlsol
0924	company or location unknown	Hawk-Penn
0925		
0926		
0927		
0928		
0929	Delaware Oil Co. Ltd., London England	Luxtra
0930		
0931		
0932		
0933		
0934		

0935		
0936	Penn-O-Tex Oil Co., Minneapolis, Mn.	Rajah
0937		
0938		
0939	Detroit Oil Co., Detroit, Mich.	Road King
0940		
0941		
0942	Pennsylvania Petroleum Products Co., Philadelphia, Pa.	E-Z-Flite
0943	Whiting Bros. Stations, Holbrook, Az.	
0944		
0945	Belgian Gulf Oil Co., S.A., Antwerp, Belgium	Philarine
0946	Transmarine Oil Co., Inc., New York, N.Y.	Pentran
0947		
0948		
0949		
0950	Penn-Ko Oil Co., Philadelphia, Pa.	Penn-Ko
0951	Penn Stag Oil Co., Philadelphia, Pa.	Penn Stag
0952		
0953	Associated Petroleum Co., Sydney (N.S.W.), Australia	Paco Penn
0954		
0955		
0956		
0957	Lou-Bob Company, Chicago, Ill.	Greendale
0958		
0959		
0960		
0961		
0962		
0963		
0964		
0965		
0966		
0967		
0968		
0969		
0970	Globe Oil and Supply Co. Inc., Wichita, Ks.	Globe Penn
0971	International Lubricant Corp., New Orleans, La.	Pennilco
0972		
0973	American Oil Co., New York, N.Y.	Penn-Amo

0974	Firestone Tire & Rubber Co.	
0975		
0976		
0977		
0978		
0979		
0980		
0981	Stephen Oil Company, Morris, Il.	Par Penn
0982		
0983		
0984		
0985	Waverly Petroleum Products Co., Philadelphia, Pa.	Evercool
0986	Delaware Oil Co. Ltd., London, England	Pennalux
0987		
0988		
0989		
0990		
0991		
0992		
0993		
0994		
0995		
0996		
0997		
0998		
0999		
1000		
1001	Erickson Brothers, Minneapolis, Mn.	Golden Penn

The space below can be used to write down any duplicate P.G.C.O.A. numbers that you discover.

Bibliography

Selling 66, Phillips Oil Company, Bartlesville, Oklahoma, 1933-1980.

Ed Love and Ollie Wicks, The American Oil Can Encyclopedia Volume 1 (second edition), Colorado Springs, Colorado, Villa Publishing Syndicate, July, 1991.

Ed Love and Ollie Wicks, The American Oil Can Encyclopedia Volume 2, Colorado Springs, Colorado, Villa Publishing Syndicate, August, 1991.

Ed Love and Ollie Wicks, The American Oil Can Encyclopedia Volume 3, Colorado Springs, Colorado, PoweRoyal Company, December, 1992.

Scott Benjamin and Wayne Henderson, Guide to Gasoline Logos, Lagrange, Ohio, Marshall, North Carolina, PCM Publishing Co. 1997.

McIntyre, J. Sam, The Esso Collectibles Handbook, Atglen, Pennsylvania, Schiffer Publishing Ltd., 1998.

Miller, W. Clark and Sabra Sonewald, An Unauthorized Guide to Collecting Sohio, Atglen, Pennsylvania, Schiffer Publishing Ltd., 2000.

Miller, W. Clark and Sabra Sonewald, Collecting Oil Cans, Atglen, Pennsylvania, Schiffer Publishing Ltd., 2001.

Pennsylvania Grade Crude Oil Association, membership list, 1951.

Notes